The glory of
Rome

To Margaret

Christmas 1975

With love Robin

The glo

ry of Rome

AN EXPLORER'S GUIDE

A. VAN DER HEYDEN
idea and photography

PROF. DR. J. J. M. TIMMERS
text

MCMLXXV
ELSEVIER · PHAIDON

Published by Elsevier. Phaidon
5, Cromwell Place, London SW7 2JL

Planned and produced by © Elsevier Publishing Projects S.A., Lausanne.
Originally published 1975 by Elsevier Nederland B.V., Amsterdam under the title 'Glorie van Rome'
First published in English in 1975
Translation by G. Kilburn © 1975 by Elsevier. Phaidon, Lausanne
All rights reserved
ISBN 0 7290 0001 X
Printed in Italy by Stabilimento Grafico Editoriale Fratelli Spada S.p.A. - Ciampino-Roma - 4-75

Table of contents

Walks through Rome	6—7	The Piazzas	52—55
Panorama of Rome	8—9	The Staircases	56—57
Romulus and Remus	10—11	The Obelisks	58
Roads to Rome	12—13	The Columns	59
Gates and Walls	14—17	The Palaces	60—67
River Tiber	18—20	The Houses	68—71
Fora of the Emperors	21—22	The Fountains	72—81
Forum Romanum	23—27	Popes are everywhere	82
Palatine Hill	28—29	Saint Peter	83—87
Temples of Largo Argentina	30	Saint John Lateran	88
Colosseum	31—32	Basilica of S. Maria Maggiore	89
Theatre of Marcellus	33	Saint Paul outside the Walls	90
The Arch of Titus	34	The Churches	91—97
The Arch of Septimius Severus	35	The Madonnas of Rome	98
The Arch of Constantine	36	The Streets	99
Gods of Rome	37	The Castel S. Angelo	100
The Temples	38—39	The Pincio	101—102
Trajan's Column	40	The Gianicolo	103
Baths of Caracalla	41	Vatican City	104—105
Aqueducts	42	Courtyards	106
The pyramid of Cestius	43	Museum	107—109
Pantheon	44—45	Statues	110—111
Towers	46—48	The monument of Victor Emmanuel	112—114
Cupolas	49	Ostia	114—115
The equestrian statue of Marcus Aurelius	50	Catacombs Works of art everywhere	116—117
Capitol Hill	51	Arrivederci Roma	118

Walks through Rome

1. **From Piazza Venezia to the Capitol and the Forum Boarium**
Piazza Venezia – Piazza Aracoeli – by way of the steps to the Capitol to the Town Hall and the Museums – Via del Teatro di Marcello – Forum Olitorium – Piazza Bocca della Verità, formerly the Forum Boarium.

2. **To the Forum Romanum, the Fora of the Emperors, the Palatine, the Colosseum.**
Piazza Venezia – Via dei Fori Imperiale with the Fora of the Emperors – To the right to the Forum Romanum and the Palatine – the Colosseum.

3. **To the Corso Vittorio, Piazza Navona and surroundings.**
Piazza Venezia – Via del Plebiscito – Corso Vittorio – Largo Argentina – Corso Vittorio to Piazza della Cancelleria and Piazza della Chiesa Nuova – Largo Tassoni – Via Banco di S. Spirito – Vicolo del Curato – Via dei Coronari – Piazza Tor Sanguigna – Piazza Navona – Piazza di Pasquino – Via del Governo Vecchio – at the end turn left to the Corso Vittorio – cross over to Via Sforza Cesarini – Via dei Banchi Vecchi, left – Via di Monserrato – Piazza Farnese – left to the Campo dei Fiori – via dei Baullari – Corso Vittorio – Piazza Venezia.

4. **To Via Giulia, the Regola and the Ghetto.**
Ponte Vittorio – Via Giulia – Via del Polverone – Piazza Capo di Ferro – Piazza dei Pellegrini – Via S. Paolo – Via S. Maria in Monticelli – Via della Segiola – Viale Arenula – Piazza Cenci – Via Beatrice Cenci – turn left: Piazzetta Cenci – Via del Progresso to the left – Via del Portico d'Ottavia – past the Theatre of Marcellus – Via del Teatro di Marcello – Piazza Venezia.

5. **Over the Corso to Piazza Colonna and the Pantheon.**
Piazza Venezia – Corso – Via del Caravita – Piazza S. Ignazio – Via del Burrò – Piazza di Pietra – Via dei Bergamaschi – Piazza Colonna – left to Piazza Montecitorio – Via della Guglia – Via in Aquiro – Piazza Capranica – Via delle Colonnelle – Via del Pantheon – Piazza della Rotonda – Via della Minerva – Piazza della Minerva – Via dei Cestari – Corso Vittorio – Piazza Venezia.

6. **To the Trevi Fountain and the Quirinal.**
Piazza Venezia – Via C. Battisti – Piazza SS. Apostoli – Via del Vaccaro – Piazza della Pilotta – Via dei Lucchesi – Trevi Fountain – Via di S. Vincenzo – Via della Dataria – Piazza del Quirinale – Via del Quirinale – Via IV Fontane to the right – Via Nazionale to the right – Via IV Novembre – Piazza Venezia.

7. **To the Esquiline with S. Maria Maggiore and S. Pietro in Vincoli.**
Stazione Termini – Via Manin – Piazza dell'Esquilino – Via Urbana with the church of S. Pudenziana – return to Piazza dell'Esquilino – Piazza S. Maria Maggiore – Via Carlo Alberto – Via di S. Vito – Via S. Martino ai Monti – Torri dei Capocci – Via Equizia – Via delle Sette Sale – Piazza S. Pietro in Vincoli – Descend Steps – Via Cavour to the left to Via dei Fori Imperiali – Piazza Venezia.

8. **From the Stazione Termini to Via Veneto.**
Stazione Termini – Piazza dei Cinquecento – Piazza della Repubblica – Via delle Terme di Diocleziano – Piazza S. Bernardo – Via XX Settembre to the left – Via IV Fontane to the right – Piazza Barberini – Via Vittorio Veneto.

9. **Between Piazza del Popolo and Via del Tritone.**
Piazza Venezia – Corso – Via Condotti – Piazza di Spagna – Via del Babuino – Piazza del Popolo – Corso – Piazza Augusto Imperatore – Via di Ripetta to the left – Via della Scrofa – Via S. Luigi dei Francesi – Piazza S. Eustacchio – Via Monterone – Corso Vittorio to the Piazza Venezia.

10. **The Pincio and the Villa Borghese.**
Piazza Venezia – Largo Chigi – Via del Tritone – Via Francesco Crispi – Via Gregoriana – Piazza Trinità dei Monti – Viale Trinità dei Monti – Via del Belvedere – Piazza Napoleone – Viale dell'Obelisco – Viale delle Magnolie – Viale Acqua Felix – Viale dei Cavalli Marini – Viale dei Pupazzi to the left – Viale dell'Uccelliera to the right – Viale del Museo Borghese – Viale di S. Paolo di Brasile – Piazza delle Canestre – Viale dell'Aranciero – Via Madama Letizia – Viale Esculapio – Viale Washington – Piazzale Flaminio – Piazza del Popolo – Corso – Piazza Venezia.

11. **The Celio, the Lateran and Santa Croce.**
Piazza Venezia – Via dei Fori Imperiali – Piazza del Colosseo – Via di S. Gregorio – Clivo di Scauro – Via S. Paolo della Croce – Villa Celimontana – Piazza della Navicella – Via Celimontana – Via di S. Giovanni in Laterano – Piazza S. Giovanni in Laterano – Piazza Porta S. Giovanni – Viale Carlo Felice – Piazza di Santa Croce in Gerusalemme – Via Eleniana – Piazza di Porta Maggiore – Via di Porta Maggiore – Via Principe Eugenio – Piazza Vittorio Emanuele – Via Carlo Alberto – Piazza S. Maria Maggiore – Via Gioberti – Stazione Termini.

12. **Circus Maximum – Baths of Caracalla – Aventine.**
Colosseum – Via di S. Gregorio – Piazza del Circo Massimo – Via delle Terme di Caracalla – Piazzale Numa Pompilio – Terme di Caracalla – Via Antoniniana – Via Guido Baccelli to the right – Largo Enzo Fiorito – Via Ercole Rosa – Via Salvatore Rosa – Piazza Bernini – Via di S. Saba – cross over Viale Aventino – Via di S. Prisca – Clivo dei Publici – Via di S. Sabina – Clivo di Rocca Savella – Piazza Bocca della Verità – Via del Teatro Marcello – Piazza Venezia.

13. **To the Island in the Tiber and Trastevere.**
Piazza Venezia – Via del Teatro Marcello – Piazza di Monte

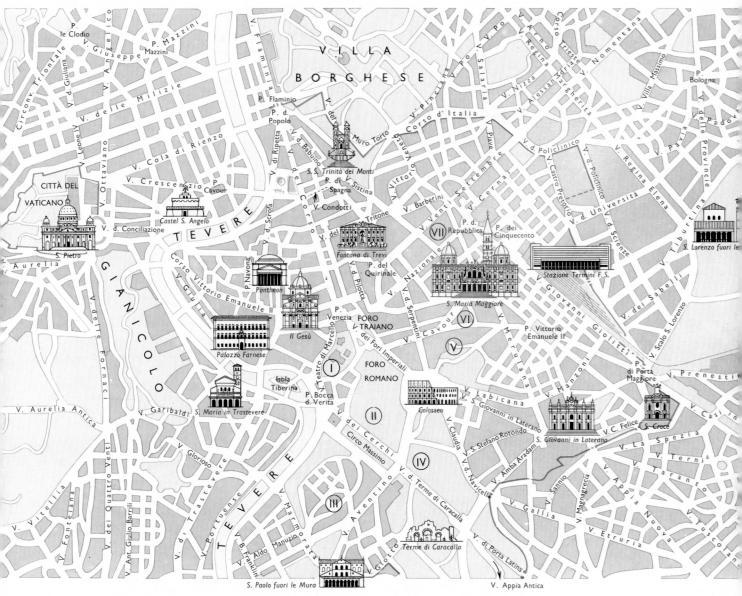

The Seven Hills of Rome are: I. Capitoline, II. Palatine, III. Aventine, IV. Caelian, V. Esquiline, VI. Viminal, VII. Quirinal

Savello – Ponte Quattro Capi – Isola Tiberina – Ponte Cestio – cross over the Lungotevere – Piazza in Piscinula – Via della Lungaretta – cross over Viale Trastevere – Via della Lungaretta – Vicolo del Moro – Piazza Trilussa – Lungotevere della Farnesina – Turn left to Via della Lungara – Porta Settimiana – Via della Scala – Via della Paglia to the left – Piazza S. Maria in Trastevere – Piazza S. Callisto – Via S. Francesco a Ripa – cross over Viale Trastevere – Via S. Francesco a Ripa – Piazza di S. Francesco d'Assisi – Via Anicia – Via dei Genovesi to the right – Via P. Peretti – To the left along the Lungotevere – Over the Island in the Tiber to Piazza Venezia.

14. The Janiculum.

Piazza Venezia – Bus to the Ponte Vittorio – Lungotevere to the left – Ponte Principe Amedeo – Piazza della Rovere – Salita di S. Onofrio – Passeggiata del Gianicolo – Via Garibaldi to Piazza S. Pietro in Montorio – Return to the Passeggiata del Gianicolo – Via di Porta S. Pancrazio to the right – Via Garibaldi – Via di Porta Settimiana – Via della Lungara to the Ponte Vittorio Emanuele.

15. St. Peter's and the Castel S. Angelo: The Leonine City.

Piazza Venezia – Bus to the Ponte Vittorio – Cross the Bridge – Via Pio X – Via della Conciliazione – Piazza S. Pietro – (to the Vatican Museums: Via di Porta Angelica – follow the arrows) – Borgo S. Spirito – Lungotevere Vaticano – Ponte S. Angelo – Lungotevere Altoviti – Ponte Vittorio – Corso Vittorio – Largo Tassoni – Bus to Piazza Venezia.

16. Fuori le Mura – Outside the Walls.

a) San Paolo fuori le Mura – to be reached by Underground (Metropolitana) from the Stazione Termini.

b) EUR (Quartiere Europea) with, amongst other things, Palazzo dei Congressi, Palazzo dello Sport, Museo della Civiltà Romana – to be reached by Underground (Metropolitana) from the Stazione Termini.

c) San Lorenzo fuori le Mura, Campo Verano (Cemetery), Città Universitaria – reached by Circolare (electric tram/bus) from Ponte Amedeo.

d) Sant Agnese fuori le Mura, Santa Costanza – reached from Piazza Venezia by bus route No. 60, or from the Stazione Termini by bus route No. 35.

e) Via Appia – from Colosseum's east side by bus No. 118.

Rome is called the City of Seven Hills, and even within the ancient city walls there are great differences in elevation. Few large cities are as rich in sweeping panoramas. The fairly steep hill in the centre of the city is the famous Capitol which together with the nearby Palatine Hill forms the ancient cradle of the city of Rome. These two hills make excellent vantage points for viewing the surrounding city (1, 3) with its massed buildings and beautiful church domes. The largest dome in the city after that of St. Peter's, seen here in the distance (1) is nearby Sant' Andrea della Valle. Looking in the opposite direction, one can see the church of Santissimo Nome di Maria near the column of Trajan with the Quirinal Palace in the background (3). The Pincio Hill is also a famous view point (2). To the south, the monument of Victor Emmanuel dominates a wide panorama of one of Rome's most colourful districts.

1

2

3

5

6

The heights of the Capitol offer
absorbing vistas in all
directions (**4, 7**). The Aventine
Hill looks down on the Tiber
and on Trastevere, with the
majestic dome of St. Peter's in
the background. Here is found
the famous view through the
keyhole, or the round opening
above it, in the gateway of the
House of the Knights of Malta
(Piazza dei Cavalieri di Malta
3, 5), showing the dome of St.
Peter's (**6**).

7

Legend has it that Rome was founded by the twin brothers, Romulus and Remus. Their story goes back to the days of rivalry between a certain King Numitor and his brother Amulius who usurped the throne and forced Numitor's daughter, Rhea Sylvia, to become a Vestal Virgin, thus preventing her from marrying and so having children who might challenge his authority. However, four years later Rhea Sylvia gave birth to twins. Amulius had her killed and ordered that the babies be drowned in the Tiber. They were washed ashore, where they were found and suckled by a she-wolf. Later, a shepherd, Faustulus, adopted them. When the brothers Romulus and Remus had grown up, Numitor, their grandfather, who had meanwhile recovered his throne and put his brother Amulius to flight, assigned

them the land on the Tiber where they had been suckled by the she-wolf. There they laid the foundations of a city, but in the course of an argument Remus was killed by his brother. This left Romulus alone and thus the city was called Rome. All-in-all it is not surprising that representations of the she-wolf (*lupa*) with the two foundlings have long been favourites in Rome. The most celebrated of these is the Lupa Capitolina (**11**, 5th century BC) in the Palazzo dei Conservatori there is a copy of it on a column beside the Palazzo Senatorio, on the Capitol (**8 and 13**). The figures of Romulus and Remus in the Lupa Capitolina are later work added in the 15th century by the Florentine sculptor Pollaiuolo. The statue was struck by lightning in 65 BC and traces of the damage are

8

9

11

12

still visible on one of the
wolf's hind legs. We know
that in the Forum Romanum
there was once a statue of the
Lupa which has since dis-
appeared. There are quite a
number of representations of
the subject scattered through
the city, for example, by the
fountain depicting the Tiber in
the group known as the
Quattro Fontane (9). A modern
version may be found on the
Gianicolo, at the foot of the
equestrian statue dedicated to
Giuseppe Garibaldi (10). The
story is presented in greater
detail on a Roman altar dating
from around 125 AD and now
located in the Museo delle
Terme, there being a copy on
the site at Ostia where it was
excavated (12). In addition to
the wolf and Romulus and
Remus the altar shows the river
god of the Tiber with a pitcher
at his side. Behind the altar
itself is depicted the Palatine
Hill, where the first stone of the
city is supposed to have been
laid. Also shown are the local
deity and the Roman Eagle,
presaging greatness.

14

17

18

19

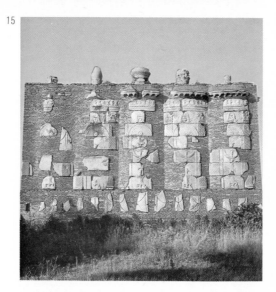

15

The Via Appia, also referred
to as the *regina viarum*, the
'queen of roads', was constructed in 312 BC by Appius
Claudius, a censor (a very
powerful magistrate in ancient
Rome). The road, which
probably followed an older
route, originally ran through
the Alban Hills to Capua. At a
later date it was extended to
Taranto and Brindisi, becoming the direct link between
Rome, Greece and the East.
In the vicinity of Rome the
Via Appia was flanked — and
much more so than any of the
other consular roads that
eventually ran to all the
far-flung parts of the Empire —
by the tombs of high ranking
families, alternating with villas
and other buildings. Many
ruins of these still exist, since
the original route has been
entirely preserved where it
leaves the city (14). The best-
preserved tomb of some size
is that of Caecilia Metella, the
daughter-in-law of Crassus, a
second-in-command of Julius
Caesar during his Gallic
campaign (17-19). The
building was made into a
stronghold in the 13th
century AD.

16

20

21

Some of the graves along the Via Appia bear busts of the dead **(16)**; any loose fragments of broken sculptures were later set into the walls **(15)**. One notices several striking monuments when starting out from Rome along the Via Appia. First of all there is the Domine Quo Vadis chapel **(21)**, built on the spot where St. Peter, who wanted to leave the city to escape from persecution, is said to have met Christ carrying the Cross. To his question: 'Lord, whither goest thou?' Christ replied: 'To Rome, so that they may crucify me again.' Whereupon Peter turned back. The chapel contains a stone bearing the alleged footprints of Christ **(23)**. A little further along are the quite well preserved remains of the circus (racecourse) of Maxentius **(20, 22)**.

22

23

GATES AND WALLS

24

25

26

27

During the second half of the 3rd century when the Roman Empire was declining and being attacked by barbarians, the Emperor Aurelian was forced to provide Rome with an immense city wall with towers and gates (24). It was the first wall to be built since the ramparts named after Servius Tullius had been constructed in the 3rd century BC (25), and much of it is still intact. The best preserved section is to be found near the Porta San Sebastiano where, on the city side of the gate, there is a decorated passage referred to as the Arch of Drusus (29), part of an aqueduct built by the Emperor Caracalla. There are a number of other old city gates in good condition, like the Porta Asinaria near the 17th century Porta San Giovanni close by the church of S. Giovanni in Laterano (27). It should be noted that most of the gates were rebuilt during the Middle Ages and adapted to new techniques of warfare. The crenellated towers on either side of the Porta San Sebastiano are a good example of this (28). Slightly hidden here by the railway, near the Stazione Termini, lies the Porta Tiburtina, also known as Porta San Lorenzo; originally it supported part of an aqueduct but was later incorporated into the wall of Aurelianus (26).

28

29

30

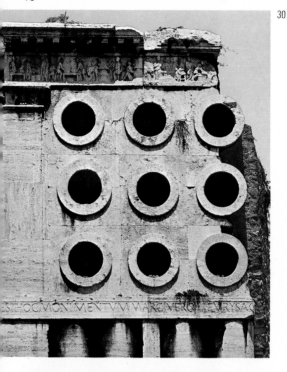

The Porta Maggiore **(33)** was built by the Emperor Claudius in 52 AD to allow two aqueducts, the Aqua Claudia and the Anio Novus, to cross over the Via Labicana and the Via Prenestina. It was later incorporated in the Aurelian wall, partly shown here, to serve as a city gate **(31)**. Outside the gate Eurysaces, a baker, had a curious tomb erected for himself and his wife in the shape of a baker's oven with the emblems of his trade in the frieze **(30)**. Near the church of San Vito on the Via Carlo Alberto is the Arch of Gallienus, raised in 262 AD by a certain M. Aurelius Victor **(32, 34)**.

31

32

33

35

The Porta Settimiana in Trastevere dates from the time of Alexander VI the Borgia pope **(35)**. In front of the ancient Porta Latina is a polygonal chapel situated on the supposed site where John the Apostle is said to have been tortured in boiling oil. The top of the building was designed by Carlo Borromini **(36)**. The Porta Pinciana terminates the fashionable Via Veneto **(37)**. The 19th century Piazza Vittorio Emanuele has a park which encloses the remains of the so-called Trophies of Marius. In the centre of the park stands a curious structure known as the Porta Magica **(38)**, ornamented with cabalistic signs and flanked on each side by a dwarflike figure **(39)**. It was used around 1680 as a laboratory by the well-known alchemist Giuseppe Bona. According to the Romans Bona's formula for making gold is contained in the mysterious signs which encircle the Porta Magica.

36

37

38

39

40

The Porta Pia was built in 1561 by Michelangelo, to the commission of Pius IV. The popular belief is that this pope was the descendant of a barber, which explains the portrayal, at the top of the gate, of a barber's basin and towel (40). The Arch of Dolabella near Santa Maria in Domnica is another remnant of the aqueduct of Claudius (41). The Porta del Popolo (42) dates from the 16th century. It leads to the Via Flaminia.

41

42

Until the late 19th century, when the Tiber was regulated to provide a constant outlet for the water, there were frequent floods covering great areas of the low-lying parts of the city. Reminders of these floods can be found in several places. The earliest evidence of a flood dates from 1277 and is located in the Arco dei Banchi **(52)**. Other indications can be found on the facades of Santa Maria sopra Minerva **(46)**, Sant'Eustachio **(49)** and in the Palazzo Corsini **(47)**. A column on the Piazza di Ripetta records the high water levels that occurred during the reigns of various popes **(45)**. Outside the nearby church of San Rocco is a hydrometer dating from 1821 **(44)**.

43

44

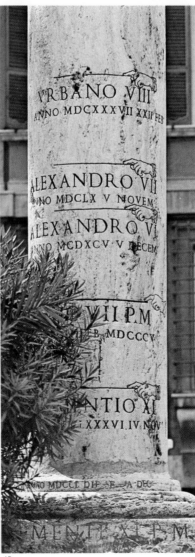

45

46

47

48

50

49

Rome's oldest bridge is the Ponte Fabricio, which dates from 62 BC and has survived almost intact (43). The architect's name is still legible (48) and, from a classic fragment (51), the name of the bridge – Ponte Quattro Capi, the 'Bridge of the Four Heads' – is also known. The Pons Cestius on the other side of the Tiber island (50), as well as the last surviving arch of the Ponte Rotto (53), are both remnants from Classical times.

51

52

53

When the Emperor Hadrian built an immense mausoleum for himself and his family, he located it outside the city limits in accordance with Roman law, and chose the side of the Tiber opposite the city, though to reduce its isolation he built a bridge across to the city banks. This bridge, bearing the emperor's family name, the Pons Aelius, remained practically intact until the end of the last century. It consisted of three almost equal central arches and two sloped arches at each end. Over the ages these smaller arches disappeared almost entirely below street level, but they came to light again during work to strengthen the banks of the Tiber. Unfortunately it proved impossible to retain these smaller arches and in each case they were replaced by a single arch, about the size of the other three. Consequently only the three central arches are original (55). The bridge was eventually called the Ponte Sant'Angelo, after Castel Sant'Angelo which explains why Bernini and his pupils adorned it with marble statues of angels. A short distance away, roughly on the site of the Bridge of Nero, the Ponte Vittorio Emanuele was built in 1911 as the most direct link with St. Peter's. It is an interesting example of Art Nouveau or as it is known in Italy, Stile Liberty (54).

54

55

56

FORUMS OF THE EMPERORS

In fulfilment of a vow he had made during the Battle of Pharsalia in 48 BC Julius Caesar built a temple in Rome in homage to the goddess Venus, supposed ancestor of the Julian family. He chose a vast site at the foot of the Capitol, just north of the Forum. He built the promised temple, dedicated to *Venus Genetrix*, Venus the Mother, and set it in a square with double colonnades enclosing two sides. Large sections of these colonnades have been preserved **(56, 58)**. A bronze statue of the founder **(57)** now graces the site. On the other side are the remains of a Roman street and shops **(59)**. Julius Caesar initiated the building of a series of similar Imperial forums.

57

58

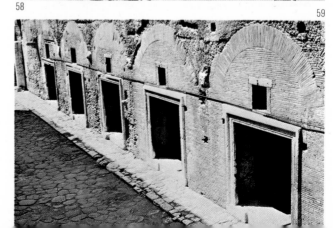

59

Caesar's successor, the Emperor Augustus, also built his own forum, as after him did the Emperors Nerva, Vespasian and Trajan, thus creating a complex of buildings whose beauty we can only guess at from among the ruins. The nucleus of the forum of Augustus was the temple of Mars Ultor, the vengeful god of war (60, 63). All that has remained of the Forum of Nerva is a section of the side walls bearing a carving of Minerva; the temple has entirely disappeared (62). The Forum of Trajan was the largest and most sumptuous. Again, only the ruins remain (61).

60

61

62

63

64

The Forum Romanum immediately confronts the visitor with a problem. What is the meaning of this field of ruins, how can anyone make sense of it? What was the forum really like when Rome prospered? Certainly, on first acquaintance, it is very difficult to see any order in the site, let alone imagine it as the vital centre of an immense world empire, complete with its temples, palaces, monuments and memorial columns, and with crowds thronging the square and nearby streets: among them senators and slaves, poets, scholars and generals, representatives from foreign lands, and later on Christians and even apostles. Victorious generals passed triumphantly along the Via Sacra on their way to the temples of the Capitol. Along this road the soldiers of Titus carried the treasures looted from the Temple in Jerusalem. The forum, in a valley between the hills of Rome, was the obvious meeting place for the people and for the assemblies of the Senate – for centuries Rome's supreme council. The temple of Vesta was here, its holy fire always alight, as a symbol of the Empire's prosperity. As time went by basilicas offered a venue for trade and courts of law. Triumphal arches and memorial columns arose and countless statues adorned the square. But there was an end to the power of the Roman Empire and, inevitably, as that power waned Rome itself declined and everything decayed—what man did not damage or destroy, time itself brought to ruin (64).

65

66

67

Situated in the northwest of the Forum, against the impressive background of the Tabularium, government archives of the Roman Empire **(66)**, are the triumphal arch of Septimius Severus, the colonnade of the temple of Saturn, which is still almost complete, and a corner of the temple of Vespasian. Standing here one has a wide view across the actual square of the Forum **(67)**. The temple of Antoninus and Faustina **(65, 67)** was later made into a church, San Lorenzo in Miranda, a fact to which it owes its continued existence, although the present combination of baroque church and temple does seem incongruous. The tower in the background belongs to the church of Santa Francesca Romana which stands on the site of the temple of Venus and Roma. In the centre of the Forum there is a stone commemorating Marcus Curtius, who according to tradition, sacrificed himself for his native city by throwing himself into the marsh **(68)**. The temple of Romulus still has its original bronze double door which dates from the 4th century AD **(69)**.

68

69

70

71

The grounds to the southeast adjacent to the Forum are called Velia or sometimes Forum Adjectum, the traditional Forum. One of the buildings that once stood there was the enormous basilica of Maxentius, completed by Constantine the Great. Three imposing arches, part of the side aisle, have survived and they give some idea of the original dimensions of the building (70). Towards the south there is the backdrop of the Palatine Hill with the ruins of the imperial palaces (73). Here the hill slopes were gradually extended by the construction of arches in order to provide more arable land. The triumphal arch of Septimius Severus was erected in 203 AD on the tenth anniversary of the emperor's reign. Triumphal arches of this kind were usually built along the same routes taken by the Roman generals as they marched in state towards the Capitol on their return from a conquest (71, 72).

73

72

74

75

76

77

The temple of Antoninus and Faustina, which faces the Via Sacra, is by far the best preserved of the buildings in the Forum, largely because it was quite early on used as a church, becoming known as San Lorenzo in Miranda. Its 17th-century facade looms strangely over the front of the temple, itself built in 141 AD (74). The former main entrance of the church is now too high to be accessible, and this indicates the extent of the change in level of the Forum over the ages. A steep stairway leads to the front of the temple (78). The front has ten Corinthian columns (75, 77)

and a frieze ornamented with winged griffins and candelabras (75, 76). The temple was originally dedicated to Faustina, the wife of the Emperor Antoninus Pius, on her death in 141 AD. When the emperor died twenty years later, it became a shrine to his memory as well. Within the temple is the fragment of a statue: a seated figure of a woman, carved in marble, probably all that remains of the image of Faustina (79).

78

79

80

81

The Vestal Virgins lived in a closed
community and their most important duty
was to keep a fire burning in the hearth at
the temple of Vesta **(82)**. The round temple
was enclosed by twenty columns. Sections
of it have been partly restored with old
fragments **(81)**. Around the elongated
atrium, with all the buildings of the
community giving on to it, there ran a
peristyle, or row of columns, bearing
statues of Virgines Maximae, superiors of
the Vestal Virgins **(80, 83 & 84)**. The
handmaidens of Vesta were revered, but if
they lost their virginity there was a horrible
death in store for them: they would be
buried alive.

83

82

84

85 86   87

The top of the Palatine Hill is approximately 100 feet above the level of the Forum. According to legend it was here that Romulus laid the first stones of ancient Rome. Some very early remains discovered on the southwest side of the hill, give support to the legend, and there is no doubt that there were people living here in the 8th century BC. Before the days of the Empire, during the Republican period, the Palatine was an aristocratic district, where the most distinguished families built their luxurious villas. In the time of the Emperor Augustus the first, modest, palace was erected, but during the reigns of his successors, palace upon palace sprang up among the earlier temples **(86)**. The principal builders were Tiberius, Domitian and Septimius Severus. The last also built the Imperial baths, on an artificial terrace known as the Belvedere, which offers fine views of the city. Although the Palatine palaces are in ruins, they are still most impressive **(85, 87)**. The Orti Farnesiani (Farnese Gardens) on the hillside are a green oasis of peace and quiet amid the bustle of modern Rome.

The Imperial baths built by Septimius Severus were supplied with water by the Aqua Claudia, an aqueduct of which some arches still remain (88). Adjoining the baths is the Stadium or Hippodrome of Domitian (90). This enormous edifice, which is about 500 feet long and 150 feet wide, was used for athletics. It had two colonnades around it, one above the other. The imperial box was built into the long southern side, forming a huge vaulted alcove in the stadium wall. An oval enclosure was later added to the south of the stadium, probably in the days of Theodoric (early 6th century). The Palatine palaces were still habitable during the reign of the Carolingian and Ottonian emperors (9th–10th century), at least in part. But thereafter, they decayed rapidly, and today only their ruins survive to remind us of their former grandeur (89).

88   89   90

TEMPLES OF LARGO ARGENTINA

Between 1926 and 1930 excavations, which entailed pulling down a number of houses and a church, uncovered the remains of four Republican temples in the centre of the city (91-95). Since the names of these temples cannot be definitely ascertained, they are usually referred to as temples A, B, C and D. Temple A was adapted in the Middle Ages to serve as a church, of which remains have been excavated (91). Temple B is circular in shape, but probably had a straight facade where it fronted on the street. Temple C is the oldest in Rome (93), and dates from the end of the 4th or the beginning of the 3rd century BC. Temple D is the most recent of the four. As can be seen, the Late Roman paving around the temples has survived extremely well (95).

The Colosseum 96-103) or Amphitheatrum Flavium does not derive its name from its truly colossal dimensions, but from the Colossus of Nero. There is a rectangular mark on the pavement where this statue once stood. It is supposed to have been about 100 feet high. In Nero's time the area now occupied by the Colosseum contained a lake belonging to the park of the Domus Aurea, the Golden House of Nero. This vast palace, built for the emperor's own use, was destroyed after his death. In 72 AD, under Vespasian, a start was made on the construction of the Colosseum, the largest amphitheatre of Classical times. It was completed in 80 AD under Titus. He and his father, both of the Flavian House, gave the amphitheatre its official name. It was designed to an elliptical ground-plan and measures 615 feet in the long, and 510 feet in the short axis. It has a perimeter of 1,730 feet and is 187 feet high. There were eighty entrances and each of these carried a Roman numeral which was duplicated on the admission tickets of the day. The building was designed to hold approximately 50,000 spectators.

96

97

98

99

COLOSSEUM

101

100

102

To protect the spectators from the heat of the sun there was an awning, made of canvas, which could be stretched over the entire building. The cornice of the highest story has round holes that could have held poles for supporting such an awning (98).

Similarly at ground level, a short distance away from the outside walls, there were stone mooring posts with bronze rings (102) for attaching the necessary cables. Marines from the Imperial navy stationed in the ports of Ravenna and Misenum, are known to have been charged with attending to the awning. Indeed, the city built special barracks for them. The Colosseum remained in use until late in the 6th century. It must have seen the martyrdom of many Christians, though

the number of such martyrs has undoubtedly been much exaggerated. During the Middle Ages the building suffered severe damage from earthquakes, the more so since the Frangipane family had reconstructed it as a fortress. In 1312, the Holy Roman Emperor Henry VII presented it to the people of Rome. From the beginning of the Renaissance stone blocks from ruined parts of the amphitheatre were used in the construction of palaces and churches. This practice was finally stopped by Benedictus XIV. It is difficult to get any impression of what the inside of the arena was like because the floor has fallen away, revealing the underground quarters. These housed the wild animals which were hoisted into the arena to be let loose on their victims.

The theatre of Marcellus is named after the nephew and 'crown-prince' of Augustus who died in 23 BC at the age of nineteen. Julius Caesar had actually begun the construction but it was Augustus who completed it in 13 BC. In contrast to the oval ground-plan of the amphitheatre, the basis of a theatre was a half-circle, closed off by a level stage construction, which, in this case, faced the nearby Tiber. The partly preserved semicircle of the exterior wall originally consisted of two sections of 52 arches each, separated by half columns **(104-106)**.

The building could house 13,500 spectators. Like the Colosseum it was made into a fortress in the Middle Ages, and later became a palace, first belonging to the Orsini family, later the Caetani **(106)**. Some twenty years ago, during excavation around the theatre to expose the old ground level, the remains of two temples, devoted to Bellona and Apollo, were unearthed. The latter had been there since the 5th century BC but was rebuilt in 34 BC. Three of its Corinthian columns have been re-erected **(104-106)**.

104

105

106

107

108

The arch of Titus situated in the southeast corner of the Forum has only one passage, unlike the arches of Septimius Severus and of Constantine. It is made of Greek marble and was erected as a tribute to Vespasian's and Titus' victories over the Jews and the destruction of Jerusalem in 70 AD. The inscription on the side facing away from the Forum is authentic. The one on the other side commemorates the 1821 restoration (107, 108, 109). The arch owes its special fame to the reliefs on the passage walls. On the left Titus is shown in his chariot accompanied by the goddess Roma. On the right are the spoils of war, treasures of the Temple in Jerusalem, being borne along the Via Sacra. Note the seven-branched candlesticks (the Menorah), and the silver trumpets (110). The vaulting shows the apotheosis of the Emperor Titus.

110

109

114

The arch of Septimius Severus, in the northwest corner of the Forum, was erected in 203 AD for the tenth anniversary of Septimius Severus' reign and also to glorify his victories and those of his two sons Caracalla and Geta (115). After Caracalla murdered Geta, in 211, he had his brother's name removed from the arch as may be seen from the fourth line of the inscription shown here (114). Unlike the sober arch of Titus, this one displays an excessive ornamentation that is almost baroque (111-113).

111

112

113

115

THE ARCH OF CONSTANTINE

117

116   118

The triumphal arch of Constantine is the largest of its kind from the classical era. It was erected in 315 AD by the Senate and the people of Rome to commemorate Constantine's victory over Maxentius, and the accompanying triumph for Christendom, in the battle of the Milvian Bridge. The arch is about 72 feet wide and 49 feet high. It gives an impression of harmony despite the fact that it was built from various parts of older monuments, dating back to Hadrian, Trajan and Marcus Aurelius (116, 119). The standard of the sculpture from Constantine's time clearly demonstrates the superiority of the earlier work (117, 118, 120). The end of Roman culture was close at hand.

119

120

121

122

123

124

125

The gods naturally occupied a large place in Roman sculpture. Their images were in many cases copied from Greek models and the various museum collections bear ample witness to this. In the streets and squares one does not as a rule find classical sculptures of the gods. In a niche of the fountain in the Capitol square however, we encounter the seated figure of the goddess Roma (121); it may originally have been a statue of Minerva. The large marble statues of the *Dioscouri*, the twin sons of Zeus, Castor and Pollux, ranged together with their rearing horses, beside the obelisk on the Piazza Quirinale, are wrongly attributed to Phidias and Praxiteles, the foremost Greek sculptors (123). Statues of the Dioscouri also crown the cordonata of the Capitol (124). River gods grace some of the fountains, among them the one on the Capitol mentioned above (125). Antique sculptures and others of more recent date are often found in inner courtyards such as in the Palazzo Odescalchi (126). The groups on the Piazza del Popolo date from the 19th century (122).

126

THE TEMPLES

We have seen that temple remains are found in such places as the Forum Romanum **(128, 132,** also note pp 23, 27**)** and on the Largo Argentina (p 30). In fact temples or their remains are scattered throughout the city. In the same way that there are countless churches in Christian Rome, so pagan Rome had its temples, which often stood side by side as on the Largo Argentina. Another instance is the former Forum Olitorium, the vegetable market of classical Rome, and here there were three temples adjacent to one another whose ruins became part of San Nicola in Carcere, a church

127

128

129

130

132

131

of very early date (130).
Aside from the Pantheon (see
pp 44–45), the best preserved
temples of the city are those
of the Forum Boarium, the
cattle market of ancient Rome
near the Forum Olitorium.
There are two in this case, and
again they are adjacent to one
another (133). One has the
customary rectangular shape
and Ionic orders (127, 130,
right), the other is round and
has Corinthian orders (129–
131). Both owe their state of
preservation to the fact that
they were used as Christian
chapels from an early date.
The rectangular temple was
probably the sanctuary of
Portunus, the harbour god,
being later dedicated to St.
Mary of Egypt. The round
temple is often incorrectly
referred to as the temple of
Vesta, but its classical dedica-
tion is uncertain; later it
became Santa Maria del Sole
(of the Sun). One of the
twenty columns is missing,
as are the cornice and the
original roofing. Consequently
we are met with the strange
sight of a modern roof
supported by ancient
columns.

TRAJAN'S COLUMN

134

135

136

137

Trajan's Column **(134)**, once part of the vast complex of the Forum of Trajan, commemorates the emperor's campaign against the Dacians. The course of events can be followed on the frieze that winds its way around the column **(136, 138)**. The emperor's ashes were placed in the pedestal of the column **(135, 137)**, and his image set at its top. It measured 138 feet overall. The shaft consists of 18 blocks or marble, each 5 feet high and 11 feet in diameter, with a winding staircase hewn through the centre. The statue of Trajan has been missing since 363 AD and in 1578 was succeeded by that of St. Peter. The Column of Marcus Aurelius on the Piazza Colonna bears a statue of St. Paul.

139

140

141

142

143

144

In Classical Roman times, the thermae served as luxurious public bathing establishments, with cold, warm and hot water baths and steam-baths. They further offered open-air swimming, sports grounds, and rooms for reading and talking. Particularly in large cities, and notably in Rome, the baths, built by successive emperors, became true palaces of princely comfort. In Rome the main baths were those of Trajan, Diocletian and Caracalla (139–141). Considerable parts of the last two have been preserved. The tepidarium (warm baths) in the Baths of Diocletian was converted into a church, Santa Maria degli Angeli (142), by Michelangelo, which allows us at least an impression of how it looked originally. In the broad courtyards of the baths of Caracalla, many remains have been preserved, among them the mosaic shown here (140, 144). In summertime, operatic performances are held in the ruins of the baths (143).

AQUEDUCTS

146

145

Monumental conduits, the aqueducts, were providing Rome with water as early as the 4th century BC. Of a total of eleven, the oldest two are the Aqua Appia (312 BC) and the Anio Vetus (272 BC). They were built underground, but by 140 BC, when the Aqua Marcia was built, construction methods had developed and conduits were for the most part carried on brick arches. The Aqua Claudia 38–52 AD which ran for 38.5 miles, is famous for the imposing march of its arches (145, 146). It had a branch that supplied water to the Imperial baths on the Palatine (147), where the buildings and fountains required an enormous amount of water. In 537, when the Goths cut off the water supply, Rome was in desperate straits. It was well into the 15th century, however, before the aqueducts were repaired, and new ones were constructed by Nicolas V, Sixtus V and Paul V.

147

43

THE PYRAMID OF CESTIUS

148

149

150

151

Incorporated in the city wall near the Porta San Paolo is the Pyramid of Caius Cestius (154). This well-preserved tomb dates from 12 BC. Behind it lies the Protestant cemetery. This quiet haven, with the graves of Shelley (150) and Keats (153) has an atmosphere all its own, rich in historical associations. Other tombs are of the German, Carstens (149), and of the British sculptors Richard Wyatt (152) and W. W. Story (155). Picture 148 is of an American tomb of which 151 gives a detail.

152

153

155

154

156

157

44

The Pantheon is the best preserved building from Classical times in the whole of Rome. Due largely to the fact that it was made into a church, Santa Maria Martyres, early in the 7th century. The original temple, completed in 27 BC, was burned down in 110 AD, and was rebuilt during the reign of Hadrian and later restored by Septimius Severus and Caracalla. It has a spacious porch with eight Corinthian columns along the facade, each 41 feet high and measuring 14 feet round. The columns are monoliths, cut in this case from single pieces of reddish and grey granite (158). The first, third, sixth and eighth columns are each backed by two similar columns which effectively divide the porch into three bays. A tall entrance with bronze doors (163) give access to a domed interior

159

158

above the first cornice was, unfortunately, restored in the 18th century. Several artists are buried in the Pantheon; the greatest of these being Raphael, whose remains were entombed in a Classical sarcophagus (**160** and above). After 1870 the building also served as a royal mausoleum. It contains the graves of Victor Emmanuel II (**161**) and of Umberto I. Behind the Pantheon — a favourite haunt of Rome's stray cats (**157**) — are the remains of the baths of Agrippa and the basilica of Neptune, a hall of 148 by 62 feet, where one long wall, with niches and Corinthian columns, is still standing (**159**).

measuring 142 feet both in height and in diameter, and lit by a single round opening 30 feet across (**156**). The interior is still largely authentic (**162**), but the area

160

161

162

163

164

165

166

167

Rome is rich in a great variety of towers from different periods: fortress towers, defence towers, house towers and, of course, church towers. Towers from Classical times are, naturally, numerous in the walls built by the Emperor Aurelius. There are also two just outside the city both belonging to the Circus of Maxentius near the Via Appia (165, also see 20). The house towers inside the city were in fact dwellings that doubled as fortresses and hail from the power struggles of the Middle Ages. Thus the family of Conti built a gigantic tower near the Forum and the Colosseum in the 9th or 10th century. Only part of this mighty building, rebuilt in the 13th century and greatly damaged by an earthquake in the 14th century, is still standing, but these remains are nonetheless quite imposing (166). A much simpler medieval tower can be found near the church of San Pietro in Vincoli (164). Along the Tiber there is another fortress tower, which belonged to the Castani (167). On a walk through Rome one comes across dozens of these old structures. It is striking, how-

168

169

ever, in a city of so universal a culture that the Romanesque and Gothic styles are so poorly represented. It would be pointless to look for a complete Romanesque church and a search for gothic buildings would yield only Santa Maria sopra Minerva. Yet the Romanesque is actually better represented than would first appear, in particular by the characteristic campanili or bell towers of Rome. These towers are built of plain blocks and are very simply constructed on the lower levels. Higher up, the lines are broken by a series of arched openings divided by small marble columns. The roof is of flat planes and is pyramid-shaped. The campanili sometimes have slabs of marble and even majolica ware set into the masonry, especially at the upper level. The plain stout tower of Sant'Eustachio **(170)** dates from the 12th century, like the more richly appointed campanili of Santa Cecilia in Trastevere **(168)** and San Giorgio in Velabro **(169)**. The bell tower of Santa Maria Maggiore (St. Mary Major), the tallest in Rome, has an unusual spire **(173)**. Its bells are rung each evening at half

170

past nine. This used to be to
guide voyagers home across
the dark Roman Campagna.
The attractive 16th century
church of Santa Maria in
Traspontina, on the Via della
Conciliazione within sight of
St. Peter's, has a graceful
campanile of early Baroque
design **(172)**. The narrow
street to the left of the church
is called Vicolo del Campanile
— 'Belltower Alley.' The most
exuberant spire in the entire
city was designed by Francesco Borromini, about the
middle of the 17th century. It
is the centre piece of Sant'Ivo
alla Sapienza, the chapel of
the former papal university, la
Sapienza ('Wisdom'). The
chapel has a remarkable
ground plan in the form of a
bee, the heraldic emblem of
Pope Urban VIII Barberini,
who commissioned it. The
spire — note the in-and-out
play of the curves — cork-
screws steeply upwards and is
arrested by an open-work
cast-iron crown **(171)**.

172

171

173

The wealth of domes is one of Rome's most characteristic architectural features. The tradition hails from Classical times and the domes of the Vestal temple on the Forum and of the Pantheon served as models for later work. The domed space always received its light from the top, but as time went on the opening was covered, by a so-called lantern using an architectural principle that also made the domes more slender. The famous dome of St. Peter's, created by Michelangelo (176), was the model for many others, like that of Santa Maria di Loreto (175) and the Santissimo Nome di Maria (174), both located near to the Forum of Trajan.

174

175

176

177

179

180

50

In the centre of the Capitol square **(182)** stands a bronze equestrian statue of the Emperor Marcus Aurelius who died in 180 AD. Almost 1,700 years old, this monument is the only surviving equestrian statue from Classical times. It was formerly placed near the Lateran and for this reason was for a long time incorrectly identified as representing Constantine the Great, the first Christian emperor, and consequently it was not consigned to the smelting furnace. It owes its present location to Michelangelo **(177–182)**.

181

178

182

183

187

The Capitol Hill occupies an important place in the history of Rome as a political and religious centre. One of its heights, the Arx, was the site of the temple of Jupiter and also of the temple of Juno Moneta. The latter held the treasury and consequently the epithet 'Moneta' has lived on in many languages to describe 'money' or 'coin'. The Aracoeli church stands where the temple used to be. The Palazzo Senatorio (City Hall) was completed by Michel-angelo and he built the *cordonata* (183), the monumental stairway which leads up to it. The main building and the two wings (which house the Capitoline Museum and the Museum of the Conservatori) as well as the square (186) are richly decorated with Classical and post-Classical sculpture (186, 187). The subjugation of the Britons by the Emperor Claudius is recorded in a fragmentary inscription (185). The halls are richly painted with frescoes (184).

184

185

186

188

Among the crowded buildings in Rome's old city there are many squares, usually associated with a building of some importance or a monument. Some squares are very old, others are of more recent date. They nearly always have a fountain, and frequently two, especially on the rectangular Piazze. The fountains are either free-standing or else set against a building. The Piazza Farnese, the approach to the palace of that name, has two fountains whose central motif is a bath-tub made of Egyptian granite from the

Baths of Caracalla **(190)**. They are surmounted by the marble lilies, emblem of the House of Farnese. The Piazza Farnese is overshadowed by the mighty facade of the Palazzo. Then there is the Piazza Venezia **(188, 189)** dominated by two very contrasting monuments: the 15th century Palazzo Venezia and the early 20th-century monument to Victor Emmanuel II. Until the latter was built, the Piazza Venezia was a fairly small square. On the corner of the Palazzo Venezia away from the Corso there used to

be a smaller building, the Palazzetto Venezia, adjoining it at right angles. It was demolished and rebuilt on the southwestern side of the Palazzo Venezia. The huge and still rather fortresslike palace was begun in 1451 by Cardinal Pietro Barbo, later Pope Paul II. Originally it was to have four corner towers, but only one was completed. It later became the residence of the Venetian ambassador to the Holy See and when Venice fell to Austria at the start of the 19th century, the Palazzo shared the same

189

190

fate. After World War I it was annexed by the Italian state as an enemy possession. In the days of Fascism, Benito Mussolini selected the immense Sala del Mappamondo for his study, and used the balcony facing the street to make public addresses **(224)**. The building, which also houses the basilica of San Marco, is now a museum of applied arts from the Middle Ages and the Renaissance. It also occasionally houses exhibitions of the ancient arts and crafts.

191

Piazza del Popolo, the north-ernmost square within Rome's walls, derives its name from the church of Santa Maria del Popolo **(191)**. The adjoining Augustianian monastery ac-commodated Luther during his stay in Rome. The central feature of this square is one of Rome's oldest and largest Egyptian obelisks. Three streets radiate from it into the city: the Corso, which runs between two almost identical domed churches, and on left and right, the Via di Ripetta and the Via del Babuino. This square, with its gateway to the Via Flaminia was in the past the entrance to Rome for all travellers from the north. Consequently many artists from across the Alps settled in this quarter, especially in the Via Margutta, which runs parallel to the Via Babuino.

Many Roman squares have a daily market. The busiest of these is on the Campo dei Fiori, where besides flowers **(192)**, they sell fish, meat, vegetables, fruit, clothing and other general merchandise. Also of interest is the antique and old books market on the Piazza Borghese **(193)**. Else-where and particularly on the Piazza Navona, art works are offered for sale **(194)**.

192

194

193

THE PIAZZAS

196

195

To the right of the foot of the stairs stands the house where the poet Keats died in 1821. It contains a small museum devoted to Keats and Shelley (195). Painter's models' were once hired on the Spanish steps; nowadays flowers are sold there and young people from all over the world use it as a meeting place.
The Frenchman Giuseppe Valadier was commissioned to improve the two sides of the Piazza del Popolo (see p 53). His work, carried out between 1816 and 1820, linked the square to the Pincio Hill by means of extensive terraces complemented by fountains to create this festive effect (197). In the centre of the square in front of Santa Maria sopra Minerva is a statue of an elephant bearing a small obelisk, symbolising the need for a robust intelligence to uphold solid wisdom (196).

Piazza di Spagna, with its magnificent stairway leading up to the Trinità dei Monti with the obelisk in front, is one of the most evocative and best-known points in Rome. It used to be the principal meeting place for British residents in Rome to which the English tea house still bears witness.

197

198

203

199

200

201

202

Piazza Navona has now been liberated from the noisy Roman traffic, a great boon to this square, which is one of the most beautiful in Rome (198). It follows the lines of the stadium built on the same spot by the Emperor Domitian. Across from the church of Sant'Agnese in Agone is Bernini's Four Rivers fountain, with the river gods of the Danube, the Nile, the Ganges and the Rio de la Plata, representing the four continents then known to man (199–202). It has been suggested that the figures are expressing horror at the facade of Sant'Agnese by Bernini's rival, Borromini (200). There are two other fountains in the square: the Fontana del Moro and Neptune's fountain. The latter dates from 1876 (203).

204

As we know, Rome was built upon hills and inevitably down the years this called for more and more specialised pieces of civil engineering, not least among them being the monumental stairways to be found at various points in the city. Another factor making such stairways necessary was the tendency for certain buildings, churches and palaces to be built on a high base in order to emphasize their importance. This was achieved, in the first instance, by raising their entrances, so that steps had then to be built. The facade of the Trinità dei Monti is a good example of this kind of development (208). The back of Santa Maria Maggiore has steep stairs as well, but this is dictated by the slope of the Esquiline, where the church stands (204). Another clearcut instance of stairs being designed to cope with a gradient are those giving access to the Capitol. Among these is the stairway leading to the Aracoeli (205, 206) numbering 122 steps and dating from 1348. Michelangelo's *cordonata* rises more gently to the Capitol square (211). The Quirinal also has stairs which link the square below to the palace on the hill (207).

205

206

207

208

209

210

211

In Classical times the Capitoline Hill – later made accessible by Michelangelo's *cordonata* (211) – only had stairways on the Forum Romanum side. There is a curious stair leading down from the square fronting San Pietro in Vincoli to the Via Cavour (209) which has a tunnel-like passage underneath the Palazzo Borgia. In earlier times this was not a staircase but a street called Vicus Sceleratus, 'Crime Road'. It is said to be the route where Tullia drove her car over the corpse of her father King Servius Tullius. The Scala Santa, 'Holy Stair', near the Lateran (210) is supposed to have been brought from Pontius Pilate's palace in Jerusalem. Legend has it that Christ mounted it and that drops of His blood still show in the marble. The faithful therefore climb these stairs on their knees.

THE OBELISKS

212

213

214

215

The squares and parks of Rome contain no fewer than thirteen obelisks. The Roman emperors appear to have had a decided preference for these typically Egyptian monuments, and employed them mainly to ornament the *spina*, the long wall that divided the circus into two lanes and created U-turns for the chariot races. Thus the m•jority of obelisks came from the race-courses: the Circus Maximus, the Circus Veranus and those of Nero and Maxentius. It was no simple matter to bring these monoliths from Egypt to Rome, a fact which led to their being also made locally. Egyptian specialists were probably sent for, and they would in addition be expected to add the hieroglyphics, glorifying the imperial power. Raising these obelisks was a problem solved by the Roman technicians. When, later, the obelisks collapsed due to earthquakes or other causes, they sometimes broke in several pieces. That was the fate of the obelisk which now stands restored in front of St. John Lateran (215). It was raised in memory of the Pharaoh Thothmes IV and stands, together with its pedestal, at 154 feet. It once graced the spina of the Circus Maximus. Bernini placed a small obelisk on the back of the statue of an elephant in the Piazza Minerva. The Romans call it *il puccin della Minerva*, 'Minerva's chick' (212, also see 196). Of the obelisk in the grounds of the Villa Celimontana only the upper half bearing the hieroglyphs is authentic (214). It formerly stood near Santa Maria in Aracoeli on the Capitol.

216

Only a few of ancient Rome's columns have survived. Examples are to be found in Via della Maschera d'Oro (213) and in the house facades on the Piazza di Trevi (220) or near the Piazza Sonnino (219). The old column in the Piazza di Spagna (216, 221), was used in 1856 to celebrate the Immaculate Conception of the Virgin. The city of Paris presented Rome with the Roman column on the Via Parigi (218). Near the Circus Maximus is a 4th-century obelisk brought in 1937 from Aksum in Ethiopia (217).

217

218

219

220

221

222

223

224

The Roman palazzi, the large residences of the nobility, developed from the fortresses and fortifications initiated by Patrician families in the early Middle Ages. These often stood in or near the ruins of Classical buildings which explains their layout: four wings of equal length around a courtyard and, in the case of a 15th century model like the Palazzo Venezia, the presence of battlements, wall passages and even corner towers (222, 223, also see p 52). Palazzo Venezia, now a museum housing important collections of medieval and Renaissance art, was never completed and received only one of the four corner towers. Its unfinished state can best be seen when entering the *cortile* ('inner court') from the Piazza San Marco; of the four wings with double arcades, assumed to be the design of Giovanni Dalmata, only two were completed. The baroque fountain and statuary date from the 17th century (226). As mentioned earlier (see p. 52), Mussolini made his public addresses from the balcony overlooking the street here (224). On the north side of the square, on the corner of the Corso and the Via del Plebiscito, there is another famous balcony. After the fall of the Empire and until her death in 1836, Napoleon's mother, Madame Letizia, who was highly respected by the people of Rome, lived in this palazzo. The covered balcony allowed her to observe the passers-by without being seen (225).

225

226

227

228

229

230

The palazzi make their own contribution to the city scene **(227)**. One of the largest and most luxurious palaces is the Palazzo Farnese, which now serves as the French Embassy **(230, 231)**. Antonio da Sangallo started the construction of the two lower floors in 1534 and the work was later completed by Michelangelo **(228)**. Once through the entrance way, which carries a balcony **(230)**, the visitor enters a cortile that ranks as one of the most beautiful of its kind **(232)**. The interior of the palace is famous for its wealth of frescoes to which almost all the great painters of the late 16th century and the 17th century contributed. The Quirinal, which served as the pope's summer residence, became a royal palace in 1870. It is now the residence of the President of the Republic. In the main entrance to this vast and historic palace are statues of Saints Peter and Paul **(229)**.

231

232

THE PALACES

233

234

235

236

The Cancelleria is another of the older palaces of Rome. It was built around 1500 as the residence of Cardinal Riario. In Napoleon's time the imperial tribunal was established there, as is recalled in the inscription CORTE IMPERIALE **(233)**. The coat of arms of Pope Julius II della Rovere ornaments the corner building on the Via del Pellegrino **(235)**. The palazzo della Consulta is situated on the Piazza del Quirinale, and prior to 1870 this was the papal lawcourt. It was designed in 1734 by Ferdinando Fuga and has a remarkable triangular ground-plan. The ornamentation is typically 18th century, rich and lively, with figures of trumpeting angels **(236)** and the personifications of justice and religion **(234)**.

238

During the Renaissance and for some time afterwards it was the fashion for distinguished families to ornament their palazzi with sculptures from Classical times. Some families were fortunate in that they could order archaeological digs on their own often extensive grounds. But not all were in this happy position and very considerable sums of money had to be spent in order to follow fashion. One might attempt to acquire items by getting to know collectors, or their heirs, or else by putting one's faith in antique dealers who were not always to be trusted. It was further the custom to have damaged statues restored which meant that new parts had to be made. The result was that, for example, a portion of a trunk might inspire an entire new statue. It frequently occurred that a trunk was fitted with a head that had never belonged to it. These practices did not always improve the quality of the statues. The most valuable pieces were usually placed in the palazzo's own gallery which would generally also contain a collection of paintings. Other sculptures found a place in the cortile or the palazzo garden. Small fragments and reliefs were often set into walls. A few of the large private collections still exist and some can be viewed on visiting days. However the majority have gradually been dispersed. One cortile with ancient statuary is that of the Palazzo Mattei di Giove in the Via dei Funari (237–241). But this is only a poor shadow of the richness of the past.

237

239

240

241

243

242

244

245

246

Among the many Roman palaces, the Palazzo Spada on the Piazza Capo di Ferro is worthy of special note. It was built for Cardinal Girolamo Capo di Ferro, and dates from 1550. Later it was decorated by Giulio Mazzoni with stucco reliefs, notably on the facade and the walls of the cortile. The facade bears famous figures from Roman history with festoons of flowers and garlands described in inscriptions along the top (244 and detail, 245). In addition to friezes with mythological scenes, the cortile contains the figures of the twelve main gods of Classical Rome (242). Not every purse lent itself to purchasing expensive antique statues. In the modest 18th-century Palazzo Corsetti, Via di Monserrato 20, the walls of the small cortile and those of the staircase are studded with smaller sculptures and fragments (246). An intriguing little fountain graces the left corner of the Palazzo Sachetti in the Via Giulia (243).

247

The Palazzo Massimo, called the Palazzo Massimo alle Colonne because of the open colonnade along its facade, is also one of the major monuments of the late Renaissance (252). It lies in a slight curve of the Corso Vittorio and backs onto the Piazza dei Massimi. It held the first printing house in Rome, founded in 1467. The slightly later Palazzo Borghese also belongs to the later Renaissance (247). It is laid out on an irregular, three-cornered basis and is therefore popularly called *il cembalo* 'the harpsichord.' The palace has an attractive cortile with clustered columns (248) and a Baroque garden with many sculptures (249, 251). The Palazzo Doria is probably the largest of the Roman nobility's palaces, and is actually a series of palaces, started in the early 16th century and added to until the 19th century. Yet in the most distinguished facades facing the Corso and the Via del Plebiscito, the elegant taste of the 18th century is seen to dominate. The cortile visible from the Corso is in the style of the School of Bramante (250). The Galleria Doria is open to the public.

248

249

250

251

252

THE PALACES

253

254

255

256

Palazzo Sciarra-Colonna on the Corso has a portico which, complete with its columns, was once supposed to have been cut from a single block of marble **(254)**. The architect of the oldest part of Palazzo Odescalchi on the Piazza Santi Apostoli was none other than Bernini **(256)**. The palazzo was extended to the right in the 18th century, in the same style. The spacious cortile is adorned with statues and fountains **(257, 258)**. The last in the series of palaces built by the popes for their relatives is Palazzo Braschi on the Corso Vittorio. It was ordered by Pius VI in 1780 **(253)** and is noted for its sumptuous staircase and the lions' heads which decorate the windows **(255)**. At present it houses the Museo di Roma. In front of it is a statue of the politician Marco Minghetti.

257

258

259

261

A villa differs from a palazzo
not only in the fact that it is
usually surrounded by gardens
— even though it might be in
the centre of the city — but
also because it generally
follows a less rigid architectural plan, as it is independent
of the fortress character that is
always to be seen to some
extent in Rome's palazzio. A
good example is the Farnesina
(259), built at the beginning
of the 16th century at the
same level as the Palazzo
Farnese on the opposite bank
of the Tiber. The Villa Medici,
which now houses the French
Academy, is situated on the
heights of the Pincio. Note
the contrast between the
richly decorated side facing
the park and the much more
sober facade that overlooks
the street (262, 263). Opposite the entrance is a fountain
with, at its centre, a cannon
ball (260) fired as the story
has it by Queen Christina of
Sweden from the Castel
Sant'Angelo towards the
Pincio. She hit the bronze
gates of the Villa Medici and
the dent created by this well-
aimed shot can still be seen
(261). At the end of the 19th
century many villas were,
unfortunately, subdivided.

262

260

263

264

265

266

267

268

269

Private houses generally do not have the ornamental entrance, the ceremonious cortile of the palazzi. There are many ancient houses in Rome, even excluding the late Classical ones. For instance, the Casa di Crescenzio ('House of Crescentius') near the Forum Olitorium, dates from the 11th century AD **(268, 269)**. It is occasionally referred to as the House of Pilate or of Cola di Rienzo. However, the inscription over the entrance gives the name of the builder, Nicolò, son of Crescenzio and Theodora. The Casa di Lorenzo Manijio is another house worth noting. It is located on the Via del Portico di Ottavia near what used to be the ghetto **(264–266)**. It was built in 1497 by Lorenzo Manilio and intended to evoke the glory of ancient Rome and to revive its art. This is stated in several lines of inscription that run along the entire width of the facade, written in finely carved Classical lettering **(264)**. It describes the house as being conceived in the old Roman fashion *ab urbe condita* MMCCXXI 'in the year 2221 after Rome was founded'. Manilio also decorated his house – now unfortunately fallen into decay – with genuine Classical inscriptions **(265)** and pieces of sculpture, among them fragments of sarcophagi **(266)**. The windows facing the Piazza Costaguti bear the inscription *Ave Roma*, 'Hail to thee, Oh Rome'. Via della Gatta ('Cat street') is named after an Egyptian cat sculpture **(267)**. Old fragments of masonry were quite commonly incor-

270

271

272

273

porated into new buildings. An example of this practice can be seen at No. 85, Via del Gesù **(273)**. The door posts of No. 80 in the same street are styled in the Classical manner **(270)**. In the old city we find stone tablets, usually from the 17th and 18th century, set into the walls with texts that prohibit the depositing of garbage **(271)**. One occasionally comes across houses with a fairly rural character, like the one on the corner of the Via di Santa Dorotea, near the Porta Settimiana **(272)**. Another simple house is that of Cardinal Bessarion, located in a park along the Via di Porta San Sebastiano. It dates back to the 15th century and, now considerably restored, is shown here among the pine trees **(274)**.

274

275

Unusual houses such as those in Trastevere on the Piazza dei Mercanti **(276)** and the Piazza in Piscinula **(281)** can be found in all the older districts of Rome. In bourgeois houses, the entrances became the focal point **(279,** Via Giulia 167**)**. The 'diamond heads' along a section of the Palazzo Santa Croce are quite remarkable **(278)** as are a number of house-fronts, richly decorated such as the facade of Via dei Banchi Vecchi 24 **(277, 280)**. Historical memories are evoked by plaques, like the one mentioning Benvenuto Cellini **(275)**. The plaquettes, to be seen throughout the restored remains of the Baroque Villa Il Vascello just outside the Porta San Pancrazio, recall historical events. This was the site of the last battles of the defenders of the short-lived Roman Republic **(288)**. The 18th-century decor of the Piazza dei Cavalieri di Malta was designed by the graphic artist Piranesi **(286)**. There used to be a curious association of wits in Rome, the Congresso degli Arguti, and at one time it seems to have become the custom to post up witty

276

277

278

279

280

281

282

283

284

285

286

SS·DOM
CLEMENTIS
FRATRIS·FILI
AC·MAGNVS·PRIOR
VT·LOCI·MAIESTATEM
AVGERET
AREAM·HANC
LAXANDAM·CVRAVIT
A·P·C·N
MDCCLXV

287

288

THE HOUSES

criticism of the government and fellow-citizens on the pedestal of a Classical statue, which has the nickname Pasquino **(283)**. This custom later developed into a series of exchanges between members of the Arguti themselves: Marforio **(287)**, Abate Luigi **(282)**, Madama Lucrezia **(285)** and il Facchino **(284)**.

289

The fountains of Rome are one of the city's truly great delights. The Fontana delle Tartarughe ('Tortoise Fountain'), on the Piazza Mattei, is one of the oldest and finest (289). It dates from 1585 (also note 470) and consists of four bronze figures of slim young boys each raising a tortoise to the basin. One can compare this perfect example from the Renaissance period with the fountain on the Piazza Bocca della Verità, a late Baroque work which dates from 1715 (290, 291). Herculean tritons, sea gods with upraised arms, support the basin which bears the coat of arms of Pope Clement XI.

290

291

292

293

The aqueduct from Palestrina to Rome as ordered by Pope Sixtus V was finished in the third quarter of the 16th century. It was called the Acqua Felice, after the Pope, whose actual name was Felice Peretti. Domenico Fontana was commissioned to design a large fountain for it and this can be found on the square near San Bernardo alle Terme **(292–294)**. It did not stand in the middle of the square, but like most of the fountains from that period was placed against a wall, architecturally reminiscent of the Classical triumphal arch (see pp 34–36). The fountain marks the triumphal entry of the water within the city walls. The inscription over the arches marks the fountain as a tribute to the Pope who commissioned it. The statue of Moses, which is said to be the work of Prospero Antichi from Brescia, is a disastrous failure. It has been called the most unashamed parody of Michelangelo's style in all Rome. The story goes that when the statue was unveiled all those present burst into peals of laughter. The sculptor is supposed to have begged Sixtus V to correct the work, but he refused saying that it should remain as everlasting proof of Prospero's ignorance. Whereupon the unhappy artist is said to have died of a broken heart **(293)**. The angels who support the papal coat of arms above the inscription are nevertheless impressive pieces. The four couchant lions are copies of their Egyptian predecessors stored in the Vatican museum early last century **(294)**.

294

295

296

The most celebrated of all the Roman fountains is the Fontana di Trevi **(295–299)** covering the complete side of a small square. It was built by Nicola Salvi at the charge of Pope Clement XII, after a sketch by Bernini. In this case it is the triumphal arch (*mostra*) for the Acqua Vergine which had been repaired under Nicolas V and Sixtus IV. This aqueduct daily sends eighty million litres of water through the fountain. The immense basin in its turn serves as a reservoir for other fountains, including the Tortoise fountain. It is a well-known popular belief that any stranger who throws a coin in the water before he leaves Rome is assured of returning to the city.

297

298

299

The fountains on the Piazza Navona represent another highlight **(301–303)**. The obelisk-crowned River Fountain (see also p 55) was inspired by Bernini **(301)**. It represents the culminating point in the composition of the three fountains that brighten this square. The Fontana del Moro to the south of it was designed by Bernini and executed by his pupils. The central figure has negroid features, which explains the fountain's name **(302)**. The statuary of its counterpart the Fontana di Nettuno dates from only 1878 **(303)**. Also by Bernini is the Fontana del Tritone on the Piazza Barberini **(304)**. It depicts a triton sitting on a flat shell which is raised on the tails of four dolphins, blowing a jet of water into the air from a conch. This white marble fountain has turned gold-coloured from the age-long action of the water. In the case of the fountain in the Piazza della Madonna dei Monti the water flows from a lion's mouth **(300)**.

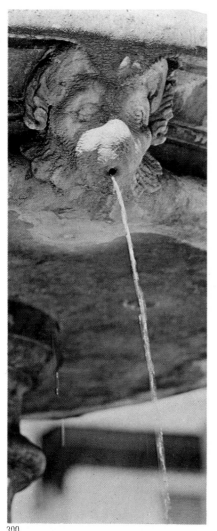

300

301

302

303

304

305

306

307

308

309

310

The fountains were there not merely to decorate and cool the streets and squares; they also formed part of the water supply (309). The fountain of the Tiaras is located behind the colonnade along the right wing of St. Peter's square (306–309). The four child figures which crown the 1589 fountain on the Piazza d'Aracoeli (305) are a reference to a similar fountain which once stood on the square in front of St. Peter's, before the latter's reconstruction. It and the fountain on the Piazza Campitelli (307) were de-

signed by Jacopo della Porta, and date from the same year, 1589. Masked heads and the coats of arms of the families who commissioned the fountain decorate the basin. The fountain on the square in front of Santa Maria in Trastevere was built almost a century later (308). The exotic form of the shells as well as the stairs that raise it above square-level are typically Baroque. The fountains in front of the Palazzo Farnese (310, also 190) each have an Egyptian granite bath-tub originally from the Baths of Caracalla.

311

313

314

312

315

The Fontanone dell'Acqua Paola (313) on the Gianicolo is another of the *mostre*, the large fountains which mark the entry into the city of one cf the aqueducts. It was built in 1612, after Pope Paul V had repaired the aqueduct of Trajan. This fountain is a Baroque reconstruction of the Moses Fountain of Acqua Felice (see p 73). A feature they share are the halls that back on to the richly decorated front where the Board in charge of aqueduct maintenance held its meetings. The Baroque elements are not only evident (311) in the generous streams of water under the arches and in the large basin but also in the greater spaciousness of the construction itself. Also of note is the fountain in the courtyard of the Piazza Cavallino in the Via de Barbieri (312). The fountain near the Madonna dei Monti (1589) is one of the simpler versions in the series created by Della Porta (315). The one now in front of Sant'Andrea della Valle (314) used to be in the Piazza Scossacavalli before St. Peter's was built there.

316

317

318

319

At one time the Fontana Paola was the monumental terminus to the Via Giulia near the Ponte Sisto. It now stands rather forlornly on the opposite bank (319). It is decorated with the dragon, the coat of arms of the Borghese family (318). The Fontana delle Api ('Bee fountain') features the arms of the Barberini (317) and was designed by Bernini. The fountain near San Rocco dates from the time of Clement XIV (321). Each district has its fountain, most as recent as 1927, like Fontana della Pigna (322) on Piazza San Marco. More fountains are found near the Arch of Gallienus (316) and in the forecourt of Santa Sabina on the Aventine (320).

320

321

322

323

324

325

326

There are indeed many small fountains throughout the city. A well-known one is the Barcaccia on the Piazza di Spagna, designed by Bernini's father Pitro. Barcaccia means 'old tub' (324). The Navicella is another ship, imitating a Classical model (326). The fontana della Terrina, the 'soup tureen,' stands near Chiesa Nuova, where it was moved from the Campo dei Fiori (325) to make way for the statue of Giordano Bruno. Sarcophagi and Classical remains frequently serve as fountains, as on the Pincio (323) and near the church of San Sebastiano (327). Nearly every cortile of the old

327

328

329

330

palazzi and sometimes the newer ones as well, has its own fountain, some of them quite large ones, as in the Palazzo Taverna on the Monte Giordano **(328)** in the very heart of baroque Rome. The fountain, built by Antonio Casoni, was in its original form supplied with water through the mouths of two big sculptures of bears placed on the top of a wall. Other large fountains are to be found in the Palazzo Borghese **(330)** and in the cortile off Piazza Aracoeli **(329)**. More modest examples can be seen at Via degli Orsini 34, the house where Pope Pius XII was born **(333)** or Via della Scrofa 69–70 **(332)**. There is a remarkable fountain at Via del Gesù, which contains a water clock dating from 1870 **(331)**. There is another fountain with a water clock in the park of the Pincio.

331

332

333

334

PIVS.VII.PONT.MAX.
QVOD.ABSOLVENDVM.SVPERERAT
ADDITO.CRATERE.EXCITATO.SALIENTE
SIMPLEGMA.CONSVMMAVIT
A.D.MDCCCXVIII.PONTIF.XIX.

337

335

338

336

339

Near the Dioscuri statues on the Piazza del Quirinale, a granite bowl originating from the Forum acts as fountain basin (337). One of the four motifs of the Quattro Fontane is the river god of the Tiber (334). In a small courtyard behind the Anima, a sarcophagus serves as a fountain (335) and by the foot of the statue of the poet G. G. Belli, a mask spouts water into a basin (338). The fountain on the Piazza della Cancelleria (336) was erected as a memorial to Cardinal Ludovico Trevisan, also called Scarampo, who in 1483 was connected with the building of the Cancelleria. The fountain bears the Cardinal's coat-of-arms, and is crowned and surrounded by the regalia of a cardinal. Another interesting example is the fountain with the books, in the wall of La Sapienza (339).

POPES ARE EVERYWHERE

341

Walking through Rome one regularly comes across the coats of arms of the popes and other evidence relating to them. The following are but a few examples: Palazzo della Propaganda Fide, Piazza di Spagna **(340)**, Via di San Giovanni in Laterano **(342)**, Fontana del Tritone **(343)**, Santi Luca e Martina near the Forum **(344)**, Santa Maria della Pace **(341)**, the Porta Pia **(345)** and finally a detail from the tomb of Hadrian VI (the most recent non-Italian pope, of Dutch birth) in Santa Maria dell'Anima **(346)**.

340

342

343

344

345

346

347

349

The site on the Vatican hill where St. Peter's now rises has been sanctified since early Christian times by the presence of St. Peter's grave. For this reason Constantine the Great had a basilica built there which was the predecessor of St. Peter's. He wanted to erect the basilica's choir over St. Peter's grave on the slope of the hill itself. Part of the hillside was therefore levelled and excavated north of the site, while the south side was filled in, to raise it up. The difference in level can be seen from St. Peter's Square by looking at the Sistine chapel which stands on the unlevelled part of the hill just north of the basilica. A series of illustrious artists contributed to the realization of the present church **(347,** with fragment of obelisk): Bramante, Raphael, Baldassare Peruzzi, Antonio da Sangallo the Younger, Michelangelo who built the dome, Maderno, architect of nave and facade and Bernini, who designed the square and colonnades. Vignola, Domenico Fontana and Giacomo della Porta also took part in the work. Note one of the large statues in front of the basilica **(348)**.

348

350

The two fountains on St. Peter's Square have the same shape but whereas the one on the north side was built by Maderno and dates from 1612, its counterpart was made in 1675 by Carlo Fontana **(350, 352, 356)**. It is striking that the upper details of these fountains, unlike nearly all the others, are mushroom- instead of bowl-shaped. They have been widely copied for example on the Place de la Concorde in Paris and in Trafalgar Square, London. Bernini's colonnades consist of four rows of columns **(351, 357)**. There are two round stones set in the pavement of the square and if one stands on either of these, there appears to be just a single row of columns **(349)**.

351

353

354

355

The facade of St. Peter's, which is a good 230 feet across (358) is articulated by half columns and topped by statues. The entrances to the narthex are below with a series of bronze doors leading into the church. The gates on the extreme right are bricked up and are open only during the Holy Year (355). At the far left is the marble equestrian statue of Charlemagne who was crowned emperor in the old basilica (353). Note especially the bronze doors by Filarete (in the main entrance) dating from 1445; these belonged to the first basilica; also, the Porta della Morte, fashioned by Giacomo Manzù in 1964 as commissioned by Pope John XXIII. At the centre of the facade is the balcony from which the pope gives the blessing 'Urbi et Orbi' on important religious days such as Christmas and Easter (354). The facade was finished by Maderna in 1614, who followed Michelangelo's original design but with a number of changes. The grandiose proportions of St. Peter's become apparent only as you approach the basilica.

356

357

358

SAINT PETER'S

SOLEMNI RITV DEDICAVIT

359

360

361

362

363

The dome of St. Peter's is 138 feet in diameter; the total height is 145 feet. It is illuminated by sixteen large windows (360). The facade (367) is crowned by statues that are each just under 18.5 feet high (362-364): each detail is in perfect proportion to the whole, as are the marble fonts borne by the figures of hovering angels (359). The interior length of the church is 694 feet (361). The nave is 90 feet wide and some 150 feet high. The bronze awning of the pope's altar is the same height as the Palazzo Farnese (see 231). In the Confessio, the area in front of St. Peter's grave is a kneeling figure of Pope Pius VI (365). The roof of the basilica offers a wide view of St. Peter's Square with its obelisk and fountains (368). The corners of the facade were originally meant to have bell-towers. The left one was completed, but later removed. The clock faces are early 19th century (366).

364

365

366

367

368

369

370

371

St. John Lateran is the cathedral of Rome, the episcopal church of the pope (369), and as such *omnium ecclesiarum mater et caput*, 'the mother head of all Catholic churches, as it says in the inscription (371). Its core is the basilica founded by Constantine the Great (372) in 326, but it has been repeatedly altered. The last re-working was by Borromini in 1650 and most recent work on the facade was done by Galilei, in 1734. The baptistry beside the church is in better condition (373). The Roman cloister court (370) is particularly charming, with its Carolingian well-head as the central motif. The arcades with their colourful mosaics were built by the *Marmorari romani*, Roman marble craftsmen of the Cosmati and the Vassalletti families (1222-30).

372

373

374

375

Santa Maria Maggiore (377) stands at the top of the Esquiline. It was built shortly after the Council of Ephesus in 431, but its present facade was not added until the 18th century and owes its existence to Ferdinando Fuga. The interior is richly decorated with mosaics, some dating from the time of construction, others from the end of the 13th century (376). The entrance hall contains the bronze statue of King Philip IV of Spain (375). The bronze cross inside the walled area to the right of the church used to be situated in the square itself (374). It commemorates the conversion to Catholicism of King Henry IV of France. The tower is the tallest of its kind in the city of Rome (378).

376

377   378

379

380

381

St. Paul-outside-the-Walls was, until 1823, the most perfect example of a large early-Christian basilica. Founded in 386 and completed in 395, it replaced a smaller church built by Constantine the Great over the grave of St. Paul. This late 4th-century basilica was destroyed by fire in 1823. The basilica was then rebuilt after the original design (383), part of the choir being all that remains of the original. As one of the four patriarchal basilicas it has a Holy Door (382). The famous marble Easter candelabrum, dating from the 12th century (381), and the cloister (379, 380) are the work of the noted marble craftsmen, the *Marmorari romani*. (See also p 88).

382

383

384

388

385

387

389

386

Rome's immediate attraction
for the visitor lies in its fountains and its churches. Some
date from Early Christian
times, as does Santa Pudenziana, where the apse has a
4th-century mosaic (385).
Santa Sabina (389) dates
from the 5th century and San
Giorgio in Velabro (387, 390).
from the 7th century. The
church of Santa Cecilia,
which dates from before the
5th century, was rebuilt in the
9th century and, later,
thoroughly modernized. The
famous statue of Santa
Cecilia, by Maderna (388),
stands on the altar. Santa
Maria in Trastevere is the
oldest of Rome's churches
dedicated to the Virgin (386).
Its 12th-century facade is
decorated with mosaics (384).

390

Santa Maria in Aracoeli, noted for its beautiful interior, stands on the Capitol, roughly on the side of the temple of Juno Moneta (see p 51) **(392)**. Santa Maria in Cosmedin **(391)** is noted for the Bocca della Verità **(above)**, an ancient round stone mask whose open mouth is supposed to bite off the hands of liars.

391

392

393

394

395

The church of Santi Giovanni e Paolo is situated on the Clivo di Scauro (Clivus Scaurus – 395) which has been there since Classical times. It is built moreover on the site of a house where saints John and Paul are supposed to have lived (393, 394). The apse here has a remarkable open gallery (395). Santa Maria del Popolo bears the hallmark of early Renaissance church building, even though Bernini made some alterations to the facade (397). It has a rich collection of works of art and there are a number of interesting tombs (400, 402). The entrance hall of Santi Apostoli is from the same period (398). There is a beautifully executed figure of an eagle to be found there, a piece of decorative carving originating from the Forum of Trajan (356). Sant'Onofrio on the Gianicolo has a small, quiet cloister (399).

It is the site of the poet Torquato Tasso's grave. The facade of Santa Caterina dei Funari (the church of the rope makers), dates from 1563 and exemplifies the very early Baroque with its sober and tasteful ornamentation (401). It is a work signed by the architect Guido dei Guidetti.

396

397

398

400

401

399

402

403

404

405

407

406

Apart from churches with domes, Rome has others which consist almost entirely of a domed space. The most famous of these is the Tempietto, built by Bramante in 1502. It stands close to San Pietro in Montorio, traditionally held to be the site of St. Peter's crucifixion (404). Santissimo Nome di Maria near

Trajan's Column was designed by the Frenchman Antoine Dériset in 1738 (407). In 1509, another Frenchman, the prelate Benoît Adam, commissioned an octagonal chapel on the site where St. John the Apostle, again according to legend, was martyred in a vat of boiling oil. This Bramantesque little temple was later banded with a frieze and a conical roof by none other than Borromini (405). It has a curious inscription over the entrance: *Au plaisir de Dieu* (406). The French national church in Rome is San Luigi dei Francesi. The salamander, emblem of King Francis of France, occurs several times on the skirting of the facade (403).

408

409

410

411

412

Santa Maria in Traspontina on the Via della Conciliazione is an interesting example of early Baroque (410). It dates from about the same period as the church of the rope-makers (see 401). The facade is attributed to Ottaviano Mascherino and Sallustio Peruzzi. The Madonna's statue over the main entrance is in the manner of Sansovino (409). The predecessor of this church was located near the Castello Sant'Angelo but had to make way for the extension of the castle's fortifications. This explains the name 'across the bridge,' though Traspontina is also taken to be a corruption of Transpadina: the church for the people from beyond, that is north of the Po. Santi Vincenzo e Anastasio on the Piazza di Trevi was built by Martino Longhi the Younger and commissioned by Cardinal Mazarin (411). It is said that the figure of a girl's head set over the entrance is a portrait of his niece Mancini, one of the mistresses of Louis XIV. The facade is popularly known as *il canneto*, 'the reedland,' because of the multiplicity and density of its columns. Sant'Anna dei Palafrenieri in the Vatican city, near the Via di Porta Angelica, is Baroque as well (412). Coats-of-arms appear to be a popular subject in Baroque ornamentation (408).

THE CHURCHES

413

416

414

415

417

418

Both the Jesuit churches, the Gesù and Sant'Ignazio, are typical of the art of the Counter-Reformation which tried, with such great enthusiasm, to give new life to the Catholic church. The Gesù, dedicated to the Holy Name of Jesus, is the cathedral of the Order of Jesuits (413, 418). Its founder, St. Ignatius de Loyola, is buried under the resplendent altar with its silver statue of Jesus (414). Set in the apex is a lapis lazuli globe. Sant'Ignazio (417), dating from the first half of the 17th century was built about fifty years later. It owes its fame to the vaulting with its painting of the Transfiguration of St. Ignatius, by the Jesuit artist Andrea Pozzo. This, like the mock dome, is a skilful piece of perspective art, a highlight of the Baroque (416). Santa Maria Maddalena (415) is a product of the Rococo. The angel beside the facade of Sant'Andrea della Valle pre-

419

420

423

421

422

vents it from collapsing by means of his outstretched wing, or so people say **(421)**. The angel is not alone in adorning this facade **(422)**. Trinità dei Monti was founded by King Charles VIII of France in 1495 and later restored by Louis XVIII **(423)**. In the facade of the Santa Maria di Monserrato a Madonna and Child can be seen; the Child is represented as working away at a mountain with a saw (Monserrat – Sawn Mountain) **(419)**. Santa Maria in Vallicella generally known as the Chiesa Nuova or 'New Church,' was built around 1600 **(420)**. It contains the tomb of St. Philip Neri. The high altar is decorated with paintings by Rubens, dating from around 1606. Santi Luca e Martina, near the Forum Romanum **(424)**, built by Pietro da Cortona from 1635, is another example of Roman Baroque in its purest form.

424

425

426

427

428

There are many statues of the Madonna in the streets of Rome, often on church facades, such as the one on Santa Maria della Scala in Trastevere **(428)**, and also at the corners of streets and squares. Some of the finest are located in narrow back alleys like the Via del Pellegrino, near the Campo dei Fiori **(432)**. Others can be seen on the Piazza Lancelotti along the Via dei Coronari **(425)**; in Piazza Santa Cecilia **(426)**; in Piazza Sant'Egidio **(427)**; in the Via Monserrato **(431)**; on the corner of Via del Governo Vecchio and Via degli Orsini **(430)**, and on the corner of Piazza di Trevi

432

431

430

429

433

436

434

(429). Despite the fact that many picturesque and charming spots of old Rome disappeared in the 19th and early 20th centuries as a result of the regulation of the Tiber and the through-ways laid right across some of the old quarters, much still remains, especially in the area inside the curve of the Tiber and in Trastevere (433). To find this one must leave the fashionable streets and investigate the lively working-class neighbourhoods. There are also areas where the atmosphere of the old Jewish ghetto is still evident, such as in the Via della Tribuna di Campitelli (437). The Via dei Coronari has reorganized itself as the centre of the antique trade (434). The Clivo di Scauro dates from classical times (436). The Casa Zuccari in the Via Gregoriana has an entrance and windows shaped like monsters with gaping muzzles (435).

435

437

THE CASTEL S. ANGELO

IN·FLAGELLA
PARATVS·SVM

438

439

440

441

442

The Castel Sant'Angelo was originally the mausoleum of the Emperor Hadrian and his successors. Its architect, Decrianus, took from 135 to 139 AD to build it: the Pons Aelius had linked the two banks of the Tiber from 135. It consisted of a square base and a round superstructure with a diameter of 210 feet. The building later functioned as a fortified bridgehead in the Aurelian city walls. During the Middle Ages it became an im-pregnable citadel and it was eventually employed as a government prison. It is now crowned with a bronze statue of the archangel Michael sheathing his sword, inspired by a vision Pope Gregory the Great had at the end of a plague epidemic (440, 441). The bridge is decorated with marble statues of angels bearing the instruments of the Passion (438, 439, 442), the work of Bernini and his pupils.

443

444

447

445

The Villa Borghese, once the property of Prince Camillo Borghese, the husband of Napoleon's sister Pauline Bonaparte, constitutes together with the Pincio, one of the great parks of Rome. It has numerous fountains (446, 447) and some, like the one of Aesculapius (448) have Antique statues. The view from the Piazzale Napoleone with the dome of St. Peter's in the distance is quite famous. In the vicinity of this terrace-shaped square high above the Piazza del Popolo are the marble busts of many great men such as Canova (444). The park of the Villa Borghese has numerous statues of poets and writers, including those of Victor Hugo (443) and Goethe (445).

446

448

THE PINCIO

449

452

450

453

451

On the Piazzale Flaminio side
of the entrance gate to the
Villa Borghese are two small
early 19th-century Ionic
temples (449). In the park's
easternmost corner lies the
Casino Borghese (452), now
a small museum devoted to
Antique and later sculpture
(451, 453, 454) and, on the
upper floor, to paintings. The
interior of the casino, which
was built by Giovanni
Vasanzio (Jan van Santen) is
also of interest, as are the
annexes, the Casino della
Meridiana and the Uccelliera,
a Rococo aviary (450).

454

455

The Gianicolo, called Janiculus in Classical times and then probably a sanctuary of Janus, the god of beginnings and of entrances and gates, is a fairly steep hill about 260 feet high, west of Trastevere. From there, especially in the afternoon, one is offered a glorious view across the entire city and the distant country. The best vantage points are the Faro **459**, a kind of lighthouse which the city of Rome received as a gift from Argentina, and the terrace near the equestrian statue of Garibaldi. The immediate surroundings are occupied by the busts of Garibaldi's followers and brothers-in-arms **(455, 457, 458)**. The noses of these marble figures are often vandalised but the City Parks Board possesses a formidable supply of marble noses in all shapes and sizes so that the damage can quickly be repaired. At precisely twelve o'clock each day, a cannon is fired from just below this terrace **(456)**, sirens wail and every Roman sets his watch.

456

458

459

457

460

463

461

464

462

105   **VATICAN CITY**

466

In the Middle Ages the popes
resided in the Lateran, but
when Gregory XI returned
from Avignon in 1377 he
moved into the Vatican
because of the sad state of
repair of the old residence.
Today, the palace is an
agglomeration of parts from
different eras, their irregularity
camouflaged by Bernini's
colonnades **(460**: also see
350, 351 and **357)**. Various
gates **(464)** give entry to the
Vatican area. Open gates have
the Swiss guard in attendance,
wearing the uniforms designed
by Michelangelo as seen at
the Bronze Gate **(468)**, the
entrance to the left of St.
Peter's **(461)** and the Porta di
Sant'Anna **(463)**. The papal
apartments are on the top
floor, behind the windows on
the far right **(462, 465)**,
facing the square. In the
summer the pope moves outside Rome to Castel Gandolfo,
a palace overlooking a lake
(466, 467).

467

468

COURTYARDS

469

471

470

Rome has many *chiostri* (cloister courtyards) and *cortiles* (palazzo courtyards). The chiostro of San Clemente is actually the atrium of the old basilica **(471)**. The picturesque courtyard of Sant'Onofrio on the Gianicolo **(473)** and the stylish little chiostro of San Carlo alle Quattro Fontane **(472)** were both built by Borromini. A particularly fine and elegant cortile is that of the Palazzo Sforza Cesarini along the Corso Vittorio Emanuele **(474)**. It was built by Cardinal Borgia, later Pope Alexander VI. The cortile of Palazzo Doria along the Corso dates from 1509 **(469)**. From the Cortile of the older Palazzo Mattei one has a good view of the Fountain of the Tortoises **(470,** see p 73).

472

473

474

The cortile of the Palazzo dei Conservatori on the Capitol houses various pieces of Roman sculpture which because of their size could not be accommodated in the neighbouring museum rooms. Most striking are the fragments of a gigantic statue of Constantine the Great **(475)**. The head is there **(476, 477)** and an elbow, a knee, a hand **(478)** and so on. These are but small parts of the statue Constantine erected in the basilica founded by his rival

475

476

and predecessor Maxentius and which he completed. (The basilica's impressive remains can be found near the Forum). The clothed parts of the statue – an overlay of bronze on wood – have disappeared, but the marble fragments have been preserved. It used to stand in the apse (which still exists) opposite a monumental entrance overlooking the Forum Adjectum.

478

477

479

A considerable amount of the Antique Roman sculpture now in Rome's museums originates from tombs **(482, 483)**, for example the statue of the man in a toga carrying portrait heads of his ancestors **(481)**. A bronze portrait head now, like the previous statue, in the Palazzo dei Conservatori **(481-483)** is probably not of Constantine (as has been suggested) but very likely a member of his family, perhaps Constans **(484)**. The Moses by Michelangelo on the tomb of Pope Julius II in San Pietro in Vincoli is one of the highlights of Renaissance art **(479)**. But there is a similar high standard in the sculpture on and inside churches, as testified by Bernini's Sant'Andrea al Quirinale with sculpture by his pupils **(480)**.

480

484

481

482

483

486

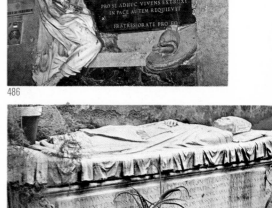

485

487

In the right side-aisle of the Aracoeli is a statue from the Capitol of Pope Gregory XIII by Olivieri **(485)**. In Sant'Onofrio we find the tomb of Nicola da Forca Palena who founded this church and the monastery in 1439 **(488)**. In the same church is the graceful tomb of the Marquise de Rondinini with a portrait in mosaic **(486)**. Francisco de Toleto's tomb **(487)** is in Santa Caterina della Rota. The halls of the palaces on the Capitol have luxuriant murals in fresco. The hall with Giacomo Ripanda's representations of the Punic wars also contains a Hellenistic study of two girls playing **(489)**. Santa Maria del Popolo contains a number of very fine altars **(490)**.

488

490

489

491

493

492

statue, which is presumably of Trajanus (494). Cola di Rienzo, Tribune of the People in the 14th century, was given a modest monument on the slopes of the Capitol (495). In 1600 Giordano Bruno was burnt alive on the Campo dei Fiori. His statue now marks the site (492). With Pietro Metastasio and Giuseppe Gioacchino Belli we enter the world of literature, in the 18th and 19th centuries (491, 496). The statesman Giuseppe Mazzini, one of the champions of the Rinascimento, the re-unification of Italy in the 19th century, was honoured by a marble monument on the Aventine (493).

With its long and chequered past it is not surprising that Rome should have a great number of statues. In the shaded Orti Farnesiani on the Palatine stands an antique

494

495

496

497

498

499

500

501

The finest equestrian statues in Rome are those of Giuseppe Garibaldi — by Emilio Gallori and situated on the Gianicolo (498) — and of Carlo Alberto of Savoy, King of Sardinia (497) — by Raphael Romanelli and situated near the Quirinal. The Gianicolo is also the site of an equestrian statue of Garibaldi's wife, the Brazilian Anna Maria Ribeira da Silva (500, 501). She fought at her husband's side until her death in 1849. Her statue by Mario Rutelli is not too impressive and has perhaps just a touch of the Wild West about it. On the Piazza Albania stands an equestrian statue of Skanderbeg, the 15th-century Albanian freedom fighter (499).

It was once considered a sign of good taste to disapprove of and even ridicule the monument of Victor Emmanuel II on the Piazza Venezia. But opinion has since shifted, and it is now acknowledged that this immense monument (502) is undoubtedly one of the most important architectural achievements of the late 19th century. The only serious objection to it is the construction material – white Brescian limestone or botticino, which does not blend with the warmer travertine, predominantly used in Rome. The statue was designed by Giuseppe Sacconi. Construction started in 1885, and in 1911, the 50th anniversary of the unification of Italy, it was unveiled. After World War I the tomb of the Unknown Soldier was placed in front of the statue and a perpetual guard of honour mounted beside it. The monument is now called the Altare della Patria.

502

503

504

113

505

The best sculptors of their time were engaged to work on the Altare della Patria (503, 506). The forty-foot equestrian statue of Victor Emmanuel II (504) was designed by Enrico Chiaradia. Before the statue was put in place a dinner party for twenty people was given in the hollow belly of the horse. Winged figures with garlands crown the commemorative columns (507) and there are others on the four-horse chariots on the corner pylons (505). At the foot of the monument two fountains symbolize the Tyrrhenian and the Adriatic sea (503). The central figure under the equestrian statue is the goddess Roma (502).

506

507

At the foot of the Altare della Patria lie the remains of the tomb of Caius Publicius Bibulus, dating from the first half of the 1st century BC **(508, 509)**. Roman law prohibited burial inside the city limits so it should be noted that this grave was originally outside the Servian Wall, which dates from the 4th century BC. The tomb was founded for him, and his descendants, by the Senate, in honour of his services as aedile of the people, an office ranking between those of tribune and praetor. Part of one of the tomb's four walls is still standing. The small building used to rest on a 16 feet high podium; which has been partly excavated.

508

509

Ostia, at the mouth of the Tiber, used to be the harbour of old Rome. It became a significant trading and naval port at an early date, and in the time of the emperors and especially under Claudius and Trajan, the harbour facilities were greatly extended. In its heyday the city had 100,000 inhabitants. The harbour's decline began under Constantine and although it was gradual its effect was final and total — all that remained of the city was eventually covered by the sands. The excavations begun under Pope Pius VII are still in progress. After Pompei and Herculaneum the ruins of Italy's Ostia Antica. are the most intriguing remains of an old Roman city. The most successful excavations, the latest, are furthest away from the entrance. The theatre has been restored and is once more in use. In the streets the conduits supplying water to baths, fountains and houses have been laid bare in several places. Many of the buildings contain floor mosaics.

510

511

513

A visit to the excavated part of the city is most rewarding and lovers of ancient Rome will gain a greater appreciation of the daily life of the period. Apart from temples, theatres and public buildings one also finds a thermopolium (bar) a fish market **(515)**, a public toilet and granaries (*horrea*). In addition to the sanctuaries of Mithras and other eastern gods there is a Christian basilica and bapistry There are fascinating streets, like the Via della Fontana **(511)**. There are houses that still have sections of their upper floors and in most, one can find mosaic floors or murals which are often in a surprisingly good state of preservation. In the streets one comes across the public fountains which served as a water supply for those people who did not have running water laid on at home. One of these fountains bears the inscription SALUTI CAESARIS AUGUSTI, 'To the health of Emperor Augustus' (or more generally: 'of His Majesty the Emperor') **(514)**. Ostia, like any Roman city, had numerous temples. The most important one, the Capitolium, is on the Forum with the temple of Roma and Augustus on the opposite side of the square. There are public basilicas, hotels (*cauponae*), and an abattoir (*macellum*).
One can wander through the streets and inside the houses for hours on end **(512)**. In addition there is an interesting museum where the most valuable discoveries are stored; sarcophagi have been placed in front of the entrance **(513)**.

512

514

515

516

The catacombs, the early Christian underground cemeteries, have been called *Roma Sotterranea*, 'underground Rome.' The name catacombs derives from a place near the church of San Sebastiano (516, 517) on the Via Appia called *ad catacumbas*, 'near the pits,' for when the catacombs were rediscovered in the 16th century this is how they were classified. Numerous inscriptions (518), paintings and other artforms were found in them.

517

518

519

Wherever one goes in Rome, in its streets, squares, parks, and courtyards there is what seems to be an inexhaustible quantity and variety of artworks. The forecourt of Santa Cecilia in Trastevere, for instance, has an Antique marble kantharos – a drinking cup – as the central motif of a fountain (519). In the Via Campania, at the end of the Via Veneto and close to the Porta Pinciana there is a niche with a large bust on the inside of the city wall, a remnant of the Villa Ludovisi which once stood there. This villa was one of the most beautiful holdings of its kind before it was subdivided (520). The name of the street to the right of Santa Maria sopra Minerva, leading towards the Corso is Via del Piè di Marmo, 'marble foot street.' The reason for this is a gigantic marble foot at the corner of the Via di San Stefano al Cacco (521), obviously the fragment of a statue along the lines of Constantine the Great's, fragments of which we encountered in the cortile of the

520

Palazzo dei Conservatori (see p 107). The foot has been there since the 16th century. The ornamentation of the wall of the Portico d'Ottavia near Sant'Angelo in Pescheria has an inscription set into it with the Latin text: Of fish that are longer than this tablet give the head, down to the first fin, to the Conservatory (522). It should be noted that in

521

522

525

523

524

526

tnose days the head of the fish was considered the best part. Attached to the small church of San Gregorio on the Piazza Monte Savello where the Jews from the ghetto had to attend a Catholic sermon on Saturdays, one can see a graceful marble offering stone **(523)**. A tablet on Piazza della Rotonda No. 63 – the square in front of the Pantheon – records that the poet Ariosto

lodged here in March and April, 1513 **(524)**. Another inscription is an example of the many prohibitory signs **(526)**. In the little Via Spada d'Orlando stands a shapeless stump of a column with a wide crack in it. The story goes that Orlando, or as we know him Charlemagne's paladin Roland, split the stone with his mighty sword Durendal **(525)**. Where the Via del

Pellegrino changes to Via dei Banchi Vecchi there is a fragment of an inscription on one of the walls recording that the Emperor Claudius had extended the pomerium, which was a kind of sacred city boundary of Rome, originally enclosing a small centre but frequently extended later on. The army was only allowed to enter the pomerium during a triumphal procession **(527)**.

527

528

529

530

531

Even church portals and those of palaces and other buildings can yield unexpected details. At the southernmost point along the Via Giulia, beside the Palazzo Falconieri with its impressive falcon heads, is the church of Santa Maria dell'Orazione e Morte, Our Lady of Prayer and Death (i.e. the prayer for the dead). It actually dates from the 16th century, but was rebuilt by

Ferdinando Fuga in 1737 into what we see today. In keeping with the name, the doorway is decorated, in somewhat macabre fashion, with skulls (528). The house at Via dei Coronari No. 45 has another interesting portal. This is the Palazzo Sala, later Fioravanti, dating from the 16th century. The doorways have been decorated in Classical fashion with Corinthian pilasters and a

cornice. Two fine pieces of Classical sculpture have been set into the jambs: on the left a replica of the so-called Eros of Phidias, and on the right the portrait of a Roman woman from around the middle of the 3rd century (529). One of the most exuberant gateways is found at the Priory of the Knights of Malta on the Aventine (530). It is the gate with the

famous keyhole (see p 9, plate 6). The entire surround of the square and also the church of Santa Maria del Priorato behind the gate, was designed during the second half of the 18th century by the Piranesi, who made beautiful engravings of the Rome of his day. The small Palazzo Corsetti, Via di Monserrato 20, is noteworthy for its collection of fragments (531).

119

ARRIVEDERCI ROMA!

532

533

534

535

536

When we leave a place that is dear to us for any length of time, we leave part of our heart behind.
Addio Roma! city of the golden heart and inscrutable beauty where the stride of the ages echoes from the sacred hills and the time-honoured columns of the temples, from the mysterious obelisks from faraway Egypt and the triumphal arches of the Caesars.

Addio Roma, *caput mundi*, capital of our world, mother of our culture. In the morning of the rebirth, in the sign of the Lamb, the colonnades of the basilicas will stand: Santa Sabina, the fair, Santa Maria Maggiore, *tutta d'oro*, all golden. Along the paths of the Lamb, the gold and the hues of the mosaics will bloom as the prospect of the New Jerusalem. New names,

new powers: The Savelli, Colonnas, Orsini, a crude time of struggle and ferment. But the Cross sits high on the Roman church towers. Cola di Rienzo tries to grasp the fasces and the eagles of the Imperium again. But in vain: The tiara and the keys and not the imperial bird, are now the symbol of Rome. Dante, Petrarch, Tasso, Raphael, Michelangelo, more new

names. From the seven hills one looks away into the distance, no longer with the arms of conquest but inspired by the verses of Vergil and Horace and by Vitruvius' laws of equilibrium, beauty and proportion.
Addio Roma, memory can sometimes be even sweeter consolation than reality.

Arrivederci, Roma! Goodbye!

Index

The figures refer to the numbers of the pictures

Abate Luigi 282
Aksum, Obelisk 217
Altare della Patria 502
Aracoeli 205, 206, 485
Arco dei Banchi 52
Aqua Felice 292–294
Aqua Claudia 88, 145, 146
Augustus, Forum of 60, 63

Basilica of Maxentius 70
Belli 338
Belli, Giuseppe 496
Bessarion, House of 274
Bibulus, Tomb of 508, 509

Caesar, Forum of 56, 57
Camp dei Fiori 192, 492
Cancellaria 233, 235
Canova 444
Capitol 186, 495
Capitol Museum 489
Caracalla, Baths of 139–141, 143–144
Carlo Alberto of Savoy 497
Casa di Crescenzio 268, 269
Casa di Lorenzo Manilio 264–266
Casa Zùccari 435
Casino Borghese 450–454
Castel Gandolfo 466, 467
Castel S. Angelo 440–441
Catacombs 516–518
Chiesa Nuova 420
Churches:
    Il Gesù 413, 418
    S. Andrea al Quirinale 480
    S. Andrea della Valle 421, 422
    S. Anna dei Palafrenieri 412
    SS. Apostoli 398
    S. Bernardo alle Terme 292–294
    S. Carlo alle Quattro Fontane 472
    S. Caterina dei Funari 401
    S. Caterina della Rota 487
    S. Cecilia 168, 388, 519
    S. Clemente 471
    S. Eustachio 49, 170
    S. Giorgio in Velabro 169, 387–390
    SS. Giovanni e Paolo 393–395
    S. Gregorio 523
    S. Ignazio 416–417
    S. Ivo alla Sapienza 171
    St. John Lateran 215
    SS. Luca e Martina 344, 424
    S. Luigi dei Francesi 403
    S. Maria degli Angeli 142
    S. Maria dell'Anima 335, 346
    S. Maria della Pace 341
    S. Maria dell'Orazione e Morte 528
    S. Maria della Scala 428
    S. Maria del Popolo 191, 397, 400, 402, 490
    S. Maria di Loreto 175
    S. Maria in Aracoeli 392
    S. Maria in Cosmedin 391
    S. Maria in Traspontina 172, 409, 410
    S. Maria in Trastevere 308, 384, 386
    S. Maria in Vallicella (Chiesa Nuova) 420
    S. Maria Maddalena 415
    S. Maria Maggiore 173, 204, 374–378
    S. Maria sopra Minerva 46, 196, 212
    S. Nicóla in Carcere 130

SS. Nome di Maria 174, 407
S. Onofrio 399, 473, 486, 488
St. Paul's Outside the Walls 379–383
St. Peter's 1, 176, 347–368
S. Pietro in Montorio 404
S. Pietro in Vincoli 479
S. Pudenziana 385
S. Sabina 389
S. Sebastiano 516–518
SS. Vincenzo e Anastasio 411
Clivo di Scauro 395, 436
Cola di Rienzo 495
Colosseum 96–103
Conservatori, Palazzo dei, Museum 481–484
Constantine, Arch of 116–120
Conti, Torre 166
Cordonata 183, 211
Corso Vittorio Emanuele 474

Dioscuri 123
Dolabella, Arch of 41
Domitian, Stadium of 90
Drusus, Arch of 29

Eurysaces, Tomb of 30

Farnese, Piazza 190, 310
Faro 459
Fontana Paola 318–319
Fontanone dell'Aqua Paola 311–313
Fountains:
    Api, Bee Fountain 317
    Barcaccia 324
    Four Rivers 199–202, 301
    Navicella 326
    Pigna 322
    Santa Sabina 320
    Terrina 325
    Tiara 306, 309
    Tortoise 289
    Trevi 295–299
    Tritone 304, 343
Forum Romanum 64, 65, 67, 68, 70, 107–110, 111–115, 128, 132

Gallienus, Arch of 32, 34
Garibaldi, Followers of 455, 457, 458
Garibaldi, Anita 500–501
Garibaldi, Giuseppe 498
Gesù 413, 418
Gianicolo 311–313, 455–458, 459, 473, 498, 500–501
Giordano Bruno 492
Goethe 445
Gregorius XIII, Pope 485

Holy Door 355

Ignatius of Loyola, Tomb of 414
Il Facchino 284

Knights of Malta 530

Madama Lucrezia 285
Marcellus, Theatre of 104–106
Marcus Aurelius 177–182
Marcus Curtius 68
Marforio 287
Marfonio 287
Maxentius, Circus of 20, 22, 164
Mazzini, Giuseppe 493
Metastasio Pietro 491
Metella, Tomb of 17–19
Minerva 121

Moses, by Michelangelo 479
Museo di Roma 253

Nerva, Forum of 62

Orlando 525
Ostia 510–515

Palatine 73, 85, 87, 89, 147
Palazzo
    Borghese 247–249, 251, 350
    Braschi 253, 255
    Conservatori, dei 475–478
    Consulta 234, 236
    Corsetti 246, 531
    Corsini 47
    Doria 250, 469
    Farnese 228, 230, 231, 232
    Massimo 252
    Mattei 237–241, 470
    Odescalchi 126, 256
    Propaganda Fide 340
    Sacchetti 243
    Santa Croce 278
    Sciarra Colonna 254
    Sforza Cesarini 474
    Spada 242, 244, 245
    Taverna, 328
    Venezia 188, 189, 222, 223
Pantheon 156–163
Pasquino 283
Philip IV 375
Piazza,
    Albania 499
    Apostoli, Santi 256
    Aracoeli 305, 329
    Barberini 304
    Bocca della Verità 290, 291
    Borghese 193
    Campitelli 307
    Cancellaria, della 336
    Cavalieri di Malta, dei 3, 5, 6, 286, 530
    Cavellino 315
    Cecilia, Santa 426
    Egidio, Sant' 427
    Farnese 190
    Madonna dei Monti, della 300
    Mercanti, dei 276
    Monte Savello 523
    Navona 194, 198, 199–202, 301–303
    Popolo, del 197
    Rotonda, della 524
    Sonnino 219
    Spagna, di 195, 216, 221, 324
    Trevi, di 220, 432
Pincio 443–445
Piranesi 286
Pius VI 365
Pomerium of Claudius 527
Pons Cestius 50
Ponte,
    Quattro Capi 43, 51
    Rotto 53
    S. Angelo 55, 438, 439, 442
    Vittorio Emanuele 54
Porta,
    Asinaria 27
    Latina 36
    Maggiore 31, 33
    Magica 38, 39
    Pia 40, 345
    Pinciana 37

Popolo, del 42
San Lorenzo 26
San Sebastiano 28
Settimiana 35
Tiburtina 26
Portico d'Ottavia 264–266, 522
Pozzo, Andrea 416
Pyramid of Caius Cestius 154

Quattro Fontane 334
Quirinal 207, 229
Quo Vadis 21, 23

Raphael 159B, 160
Romulus and Remus 9–12

Sapienza 339
Scala Santa 210
Septimius Severus, Arch of 111–115
Servius Tullius, Walls of 25
Skanderbeg 499
Speaking Statues 282, 283, 284, 285, 287
Swiss Guards 461, 463, 468

Temple,
    Antoninus and Faustina 65, 67
    Apollo 104, 106
    Boarium 127, 129–133
    Largo Argentina 91, 95
    Mars Ultor 60, 63
    Romulus 69
    Vesta 132, 133
Tiber 43
Titus, Arch of 107–110
Trajan 494
Trajan, Column of 134–138
Trajan, Forum of 58, 59, 61
Trinita dei Monti 208, 423

Unknown Soldier, Tomb of 502
Urbi et Orbi 354

Vatican City 460–465
Via,
    Appia 14–19
    Banchi Vecchi, dei 277, 280
    Campania 520
    Coronari, dei 425, 434, 529
    Funari, dei 237–241
    Gesù, del 270, 273, 331
    Giulia 243, 279, 528
    Gregoriana 435
    Maschera d'Oro, della 213
    Monserrato, di 246, 430, 531
    Orsini, degli 333, 431
    Parigi 218
    Pellegrino, del 235, 429, 527
    Pie' di Marmo, del 521
    Plebiscito, del 225
    San Giovanni in Laterano, di 342
    Santa Dorotea 272
    Scrofa, della 332
    Spada d'Orlando 525
    Tribuna di Campitelli 437

Victor Emmanuel II 161, 502–507
Victor Hugo 443
Villa,
    Borghese 446–449
    Celimontana 214
    Farnesina 259
    Il Vascello 288
    Ludovisi 520
    Medici 260–263